Pan/Ballantine

Graeme Kent

Guadalcanal: island ordeal

Editor-in-Chief: Barrie Pitt
Editor: David Mason
Art Director: Sarah Kingham
Picture Editor: Robert Hunt
Designer: David Allen
Cover: Denis Piper
Special Drawings: John Batchelor
Photographic Research: Benedict Shephard
Cartographer: Richard Natkiel

Photographs for this book were especially selected from the following archives: 8–9 US National Archives; 12–13 Keystone Press; 14–15 US National Archives; 16–17 Popperfoto; 19 Associated Press; 19–20 US National Archives; 23 US Army; 23 US Marine Corps; 23 US National Archives; 25 US Air Force; 25 US National Archives; 25 Imperial War Museum; 25–29 US National Archives; 30 IWM; 31 US National Archives; 34 Associated Press; 34–35 IWM; 36 US National Archives; 36 IWM; 38–39 Keystone; 40–41 US National Archives; 42–46 US National Archives; 46 Australian War Memorial; 48–49 US National Archives; 49 US Navy; 50–51 US National Archives; 50 US Navy; 51 US National Archives; 52–53 Associated Press; 56–58 US Marine Corps; 62–63 US National Archives; 66 IWM; 66 US National Archives; 67 US Navy; 68 US National Archives; 68 IWM; 69–75 US National Archives; 76–77 Keystone; 77–78 US National Archives; 79 US Marine Corps; 82–83 Keystone; 84–86 US National Archives; 86 US Navy; 87 US National Archives; 88 IWM; 88 Keystone; 89 US Marine Corps; 90–97 Keystone; 98–105 US National Archives; 105 US Navy; 108 US National Archives; 108 US Navy; 109–111 US National Archives; 112–113 US Marine Corps; 114 US Army; 114–119 US Marine Corps; 120 Popperfoto; 120–123 US National Archives; 124 US Marine Corps; 128–129 US National Archives; 129 US Air Force; 130 US Marine Corps; 132–134 US National Archives; 134 US Army; 135 Associated Press; 136–137 US Army; 138–139 US Air Force; 142–143 Keystone; 142–143 US Army; 143 US Navy; 146–147 US Army; 147 US Marine Corps; 148–149 US Army; 150 US Marine Corps; 152–155 US National Archives; 156–157 US Air Force; 158 US Marine Corps; 159 Camera Press; front cover Central Press Ltd; back cover Keystone.

Contents

Springboard.

Introduction by Barrie Pitt

Chroniclers of human conflict have always been adept at finding reasons for the campaign they are involved in to be considered the uniquely critical one. Partly this is a concession to the reader, who would naturally rather have the sense of being present at a particularly dramatic juncture, and partly it is due to the fact that military writers, like other professionals, have their own specialities; and specialists commonly accord their own niche an importance which the rest of us find exaggerated.

The war in the Pacific has proved fertile ground for the martial tiller, throwing up a literary crop abounding in superlatives. But there are, in this case, very good reasons. The Pacific theatre was so vast, the nature of the war so unprecedented and the contingencies encountered so varied that each episode can genuinely claim to be of peculiar interest in some way shared by no other. And in the forefront of the many acts in that potent drama stands the campaign for Guadalcanal.

Graeme Kent places the campaign firmly in its rightful place. It enshrines, as he points out in a narrative of great clarity, a number of 'firsts' for which it would be notable had it no other claims to fame. It was, for instance, the first amphibious landing made by US forces since 1898 – and there cannot have been many surviving in the American military world who had even the dubious advantage of that prior experience to draw upon. In the Guadalcanal landings therefore, virtually every decision and every tactical move was essentially an experiment; in the circumstances it is

not surprising that a certain amount of confusion characterised the operation. It was certainly a far cry from the highly systematized and efficient later assault landings in the Pacific, but it was a signal – if not unqualified – success, and the lessons were well learned.

The subsequent struggle for the island is chiefly remembered for being first in another respect however. It saw for the first time, in a succession of unprecedented territorial conquests, the 'unbeatable' Japanese invader soundly and spectacularly beaten and forced into ignominious retreat. Not that this had suddenly become an easy accomplishment. On the contrary, the Japanese fought as they always had: with complete dedication, bravery and a sustained ferocity which ceased only with total defeat. Losses, on both sides, were eclipsed by the losses of later campaigns, but for sheer savagery the fighting on and around Guadalcanal was never surpassed. The variety of the action, too, was enormous, and was to become typical of the island campaigns. At one and the same time there could well be every conceivable kind of battle in progress. A naval action might coincide with a shore bombardment while overhead bombers droned and both carrier-borne and land based fighters, dive bombers and torpedo planes contested for mastery; and on land battles ranging in scale from engagements involving thousands to small guerilla actions could be adding their noise to the din.

This relatively unimportant island in the Solomons became for the

6

Japanese and Americans alike a symbol, the struggle to possess it a test case; and it grew to be a classic example of what everyone knows now as 'escalation'. The campaign took on some of the character of a grim and ruthless auction, each bidder hardening in his resolve, recklessly raising the price as his opponent threatened to outbid him; meanwhile the value of the article itself faded into the background as the contest became its own *raison d'être*.

Time after time reinforcements poured in for the Japanese via the 'Tokyo Express' and in response further men and materiel arrived to strengthen the Allied position. Numbers of aircraft and ships involved rose to new heights, the conflict became more bitter, more intense.

The longer such a process continues of course, the greater become both the eventual triumph of the victor and the humiliation of the loser; neither combatant could contemplate being in the latter position. This was well understood in the Pacific, in America and in Japan. So when eventually Guadalcanal was taken it was clear that the US forces had survived and overcome despite the worst that the Japanese, at full stretch, could fling against them. The balance of morale in the Pacific and southeast Asia swung significantly for the first time in favour of the Allies – and from that moment the Japanese were fighting a defensive war.

A factor of great importance which worked against the Japanese in the Solomons and on other occupied island groups was the arrogant insensitivity they thought a proper attitude to adopt towards native populations. In order, it seems, merely to display their imagined superiority they ill-treated and exploited their 'subjects' and wantonly destroyed the gardens which were often the natives' sole livelihood. Instead, however, of being cowed by this treatment, the proud and independant islanders quickly developed an active loathing for their masters and seized every opportunity to sabotage their operations. In conjunction with the Coastwatchers they formed efficient spy and liaison networks which contributed in no small measure to the efficiency of Allied planning. Even so, the surprise evacuation of the remnants of the Japanese land force, one of the most efficiently organised operations of the Pacific War, was accomplished somehow in perfect secrecy.

The hopeless effort of the Japanese bid to retake Guadalcanal – Operation *Ka* – was as much the failure of an attitude of mind as one of resources. The willingness of the Japanese fighting man to sacrifice himself without second thought was the positive side of a coin whose reverse was the unthinking wastage of valuable lives in hopeless missions. When defeat is certain,as here in the long run it was bound to be once America's enormous industrial potential became geared to all-out war, the courage which results in even more complete defeat ceases to have value. Throwing good money after bad has never been a policy noted for success. Sadly, however, it is one which takes hard lessons to unlearn.

'Japani come'

launched their first successful offensive against the Japanese.

The total casualties for this campaign have never been fully established. Of the Japanese land forces alone between 21,000 and 28,500 men died in a little over five months, justifying the claim of one of its generals that the Japanese army lay buried in the graveyard of Guadalcanal. The American land forces dead came to over 1,500, while many more naval personnel were killed off the shores of the island. The attitude of the fighting men to their dreadful surroundings is summed up in a piece of doggerel popular among American Marines at the time:

And when he gets to Heaven
To St Peter he will tell:
'One more Marine reporting, sir –
I've served my time in Hell!'

The Solomons extend in a straggling south-easterly chain over 900 miles long between Papua, New Guinea and the New Hebrides. They form part of a scattered necklace of islands across the Pacific to the north-east of Australia. There are six major islands, of which Guadalcanal is the largest, and many smaller ones. The terrain is generally mountainous with dense jungles. Both heat and humidity are high and there are fierce tropical rainstorms; rainfall of over 200 inches has been recorded in one year.

The majority of Solomon Islanders are Melanesians, with some Polynesians and a few Micronesians. They are a reserved and intelligent people, stubbornly independent and jealous of their land-rights. They live in small, close-knit communities. Over sixty languages are spoken among 160,000 people and there is a long tradition of inter-island and even inter-village warfare. Before the Second World War, as today, most of the islanders lived by tending their gardens, growing kumura, taro, yams and fruit, and by fishing.

When the novelist Jack London visited the Solomon Islands in 1908 he called them 'as near the rawest edge of screaming savagery as any place on this earth'. Thirty-four years later American and Japanese troops on Guadalcanal were to provide an exhibition of vicious hand to hand combat which made the head-hunting exploits of the old days seem tame by comparison. For a few months the name of Guadalcanal was seldom out of the headlines. It became a synonym for desperate fighting under atrocious conditions. Today the island is recognised as having been the turning-point of the Pacific campaign and the springboard from which the Allies

9

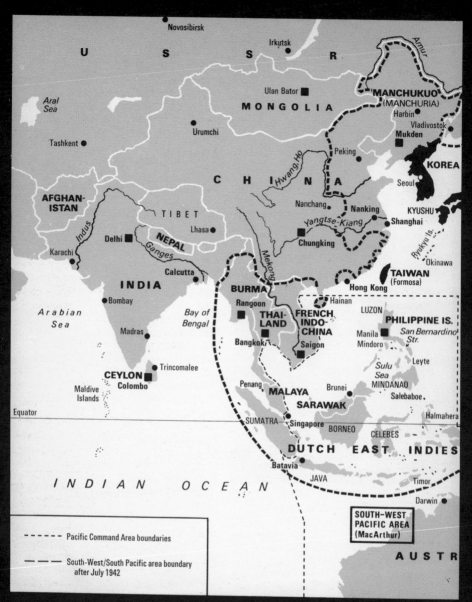

The Pacific Theatre in 1942

Tulagi, capital of the Solomon Islands, from the sea

Nominally administered by Great Britain but possessing few natural resources and with copra as the only cash crop of note, little had been done to develop the Protectorate before 1942. A handful of district officers maintained law and order among the salt water and bush villages, while some European missionaries, planters, traders and soldiers of fortune were also in evidence. The islands, often beautiful, usually fascinating, were a backwater.

Then war came to the Solomons and for the first time in its history the Protectorate was of importance to the outside world. Since Pearl Harbor the Japanese had been advancing remorselessly. They had taken Guam, Hong Kong, the Philippines, Singapore and the Dutch East Indies. In January they had occupied Rabaul in New Guinea. Bougainville was seized in March. Then the Japanese invaded the British Solomon Islands Protectorate.

By an accident of geography the islands lay across the path of any Japanese progress towards Australia or Hawaii. With the New Hebrides and Fiji they formed part of the precious Allied lines of communication. They also provided a logical area for any American counter-attack.

On 5th March 1942, Admiral Ernest King, Cominch (Commander-in-Chief) United States Fleet, informed President Roosevelt of his intentions in pursuing the war in the Pacific. These were to hold Hawaii, support Australasia and to drive north-westwards from the New Hebrides. This third endeavour would consist of an attack launched from Guadalcanal against the Japanese entrenched at Rabaul.

By this time the Japanese were well on their way to the Solomons. By July

at the small seaplane base near Tulagi, and a hastily recruited Solomon Islands Defence Force.

This latter organisation consisted originally of three officers, two NCOs and 112 native other ranks, largely recruited from the local constabulary. Eventually all the remaining British administrative officers were given commissioned rank in this force.

One other organisation was recruited – the coastwatchers. These men, government officers, Australian planters and traders, volunteered to live behind the Japanese lines and transmit information on enemy shipping and aircraft movements. Organised from New Guinea by Lieutenant-Commander Eric Feldt of the Royal Australian Navy, the coastwatchers provided a vital chain of intelligence agents among the Pacific islands. Each man was equipped with an AWA teleradio, a transmitter/receiver with four alternative transmission frequencies and with a range of four hundred to six hundred miles.

Among the first coastwatchers to be appointed in the Solomons were Kennedy in the West, Wilson in the East and Forster on San Cristobal. By virtue of its location in the Central Solomons Guadalcanal was obviously going to be of strategic importance. It was supplied with three coastwatchers. Martin Clemens, a young district officer took up position at the village of Aola, a district sub-station on the north coast of the island. D S Macfarlan, a lieutenant in the Royal Australian Naval Reserve, made an initial camp near Lunga opposite Tulagi. Later he moved inland to Gold Ridge. Here he found already installed K D Hay, a planter, and A M Andersen, a gold miner. On the west coast of Guadalcanal the third coastwatcher, F A 'Snowy' Rhoades, a former plantation manager, settled down to await the arrival of the Japanese.

All these movements had been made in some haste because by March regular Japanese bombing raids were

Guadalcanal had been occupied by troops of the 81st and 84th Garrison Units and 11th and 13th Naval Construction Battalions of the 8th Base Force. The Japanese advance into the Protectorate was virtually unimpeded. The Resident Commissioner, William Marchant, had remained at his post with a few volunteers from his staff, while missionaries of all faiths had also elected to stay. Most of the Europeans, however, had been evacuated on the vessel *Morinda* from Tulagi, the headquarters of the British administration. Tulagi was situated on the island of Ngela, opposite Guadalcanal.

At the time of the Japanese invasion there was only a token armed force in the islands and resistance would plainly have been useless. There were a few riflemen of the Australian Imperial Force and some RAAF personnel servicing occasional Catalina flying boats on refuelling stops

already being made on Tulagi. The Resident Commissioner moved his headquarters to the island of Malaita, where he remained undisturbed. While awaiting the inevitable Japanese invasion he sent his officers round the islands to talk to the inhabitants. Their message was a simple one. It was possible that the enemy would arrive soon. Nevertheless the islands were British and would remain so. No Solomon Islander was to offer help to the Japanese.

There was one other important administrative chore to be accomplished. Many labourers had been stranded on plantations far from home. Their return was accomplished in two weeks by the use of a fleet of schooners. These vessels were sometimes bombed but every labourer was returned to his own island.

On 10th April the Japanese landed in the Shortland Islands in the Western

Solomons. The occupation of the rest of the Protectorate seemed imminent. Bombing raids on Tulagi increased in intensity. On 2nd May there were five heavy attacks in one day.

The following morning a Japanese naval unit under the command of Rear-Admiral Goto berthed unopposed in Tulagi harbour. Among the force disembarked from the ships were the Yokohama Air Group, the Third Kure Special Navy Landing Force, a naval seaplane base unit, an anti-aircraft battery and various radio communications personnel. Twelve Kawanishi seaplanes and a dozen Zero floatplanes arrived later.

The Japanese were not allowed to settle at Tulagi unmolested, although the American attack which occurred was somewhat fortuitous. On 4th May, while Goto was still unloading supplies, his ships were attacked by aircraft from the US light carriers

Left: Martin Clemens, who acted as a coastwatcher throughout the Japanese occupation, with native scouts.
Above: Admiral Fletcher

Lexington and *Yorktown*.

These vessels were part of Task Force 17, led by Rear Admiral F J Fletcher. Fletcher was on his way to intercept a Japanese landing force reported heading through the Coral Sea in the direction of Port Moresby. Aircraft from his carriers spotted the Japanese moored at Tulagi and went in to the attack. A considerable number of bombs were dropped and a great deal of ammunition expended. Exaggerated claims were made for the success of this mission, but when the attack was over only the destroyer *Kikutsuki*, two small minesweepers and a number of seaplanes had been destroyed.

This was the last reverse the Japanese were to suffer for some months in the Solomons. They proceeded to dig in on Tulagi. On Guadalcanal and other islands coastwatchers built up supplies of food and continued to warn the natives not to collaborate.

At Aola Martin Clemens had gathered around him a private force of some sixty natives, among whom he shared the twelve rifles in his possession. Later his men retrieved another six rifles and 2,500 rounds of ammunition abandoned by the Australians before they had left the Solomons. Clemens also established a fleet of canoes. The men of one of the canoes reported that the Japanese seemed to be preparing to move over to Guadalcanal. Two weeks later, on 28th May an exploratory Japanese force landed at Lunga Point. Clemens moved inland to the village of Vungana, continuing to send out patrols and maintain a tree-top vigil.

On 1st July one of Clemens' scouts, Dovu, came with the news the coastwatcher had been expecting and fearing: 'Japani come'. The Japanese had landed in force on Guadalcanal. Now all that Clemens could do was to watch and hope that the Americans in their turn were making plans to invade Guadalcanal.

Operation
Watchtower

Transports of the US invasion force on their way to Guadalcanal

Harbor. Their findings had been confirmed early in 1942 by President Roosevelt and Mr Churchill. If the Japanese entered the war they would be contained in the Pacific until the fighting in Europe was over.

Such a policy did not allow for the strong personalities of the men entrusted with conducting the Allied campaign in the Pacific, or with the influences motivating them. The USA was smarting from a series of reverses. The reputation of the American fighting man had been denied in no uncertain terms by the Japanese. A significant victory was needed to restore morale at home and among the fighting services.

This point was urged by the three men most intimately concerned with planning operations in the Pacific: General Douglas MacArthur, Admiral Ernest King and Admiral Chester W Nimitz. Each man was a personality in his own right. MacArthur after his well-publicised escape from Corregidor and with his flair for the dramatic was perhaps the best known, but King, a tough, humourless character who was reputed to shave with a blow-torch, was no less hard. The white-haired Nimitz, although tending to be overshadowed by the other two, was an efficient and experienced career officer

On the 4th April the Joint Chiefs of Staff divided the Pacific area between MacArthur and Nimitz. The dividing line was decided at 160 degrees east longitude. This meant that MacArthur had responsibility for the south-west, which included Australia, New Guinea, the Philippines and the Solomons, while Nimitz assumed control of the rest. (Four months later, with 'Operation Watchtower', the assault on the Solomons, about to take place as a Naval and Marine operation, this line was adjusted one degree to the west so that Nimitz received the whole of Guadalcanal, Tulagi and the

Guadalcanal was not the most urgent concern of the Joint Chiefs of Staff at the beginning of 1942. There were other islands as important and these had to be occupied and fortified before there could be any thought of attack. Mixed US army and navy forces started to go ashore at a number of islands not yet within the Japanese sphere of influence. Samoa and Fiji were garrisoned. On 12th March Noumea in New Caledonia was occupied. Two weeks later the 4th Defence Battalion (Reinforced) Fleet Marine Force took over at Port Vila in the New Hebrides.

A holding operation was what seemed called for. This had been decided at meetings of the British and US military staffs long before Pearl

17

Floridas as well.)

Dissension raged among the members of the JCS about the tactics to be employed in the Pacific. From Washington, General George C Marshall, the US Army Chief of Staff, wanted to adhere to the original conception that 'the military strategy in the Far East will be defensive.' He was backed by General H H Arnold, chief of the Army Air Force. MacArthur and King disagreed vehemently with this attitude; unfortunately there was little unanimity in their dissension. King advocated a limited offensive in the area of Guadalcanal and Tulagi, supported from the air by army B-17s and navy PBYs flying from the newly constructed airfield at Espiritu Santo in the New Hebrides. On 28th May, Nimitz suggested a modification of this plan – to take and raze Tulagi with a single Raider battalion. This proposal was vetoed by Marshall, MacArthur and King on the grounds of impracticability.

On the 4th and 5th of June, aircraft from US aircraft carriers sank four Japanese carriers off Midway. This success inspired MacArthur to urge a direct attack on Rabaul. He was convinced that Rabaul could be taken in July by a division trained in amphibious warfare and carried in twelve transports backed by two carriers and a number of bombers. This plan had the support of General Marshall who envisaged the First Marine Division making the initial beachhead landing and then being relieved by two United States and one Australian division.

Admiral King refused to give this project his backing, declaring that fighter aircraft would also be necessary for this venture to succeed, and that it would be foolhardy to risk two of the aircraft carriers available on such a hazardous expedition. King then issued a counter-proposal – attacks on Tulagi – Guadalcanal and also on the Santa Cruz group in the Eastern Solomons while General MacArthur led a feint in the Dutch East Indies.

This last suggestion was deemed too ambitious, but King pressed energetically for an attack on Tulagi and Guadalcanal, especially as coastwatchers had reported that the Japanese were now building an airfield on the latter island. Finally the admiral had his way. Overcoming the opposition of Marshall and MacArthur, he received their grudging assent to his plan. The Joint Chiefs of Staff ordered the operation to take place. King at once passed on the order to Nimitz, who had been given command of Task I of Operation Watchtower, the initial attack. General MacArthur was to be entrusted with Task II, the seizure of the Northern Solomons, and Task III, the attack on Rabaul. Nimitz in turn briefed Vice-Admiral Robert L Ghormley, who had been appointed the navy's commander in the South Pacific. Ghormley was not pleased at being brought into the picture so late in the proceedings. Little time was left for the collection of intelligence and planning of operations. Admiral King, however, was adamant; he had secured the Tulagi-Guadalcanal mission as a naval project, now it was up to Ghormley and Nimitz.

On 26th June in Auckland, New Zealand, Vice-Admiral Ghormley informed General Alexander Archer Vandegrift, commander of the First Marine Division that he was to lead the amphibious assault on Tulagi and Guadalcanal on 1st August – less than five weeks away. Vandegrift, a quiet, courteous Virginian with thirty-three years' service, was considerably shaken at the short notice. He had been in New Zealand only twelve days. Less than half his division was with him. His 1st Regiment was somewhere in the Pacific, having left San Francisco only four days earlier in eight cargo ships. The 7th Marines were on Samoa.

In vain Vandegrift expostulated that he had not expected to be called into action until early 1943. Ghormley liked the situation as little as the

General Douglas MacArthur in 1942   Admiral Chester W Nimitz in 1942

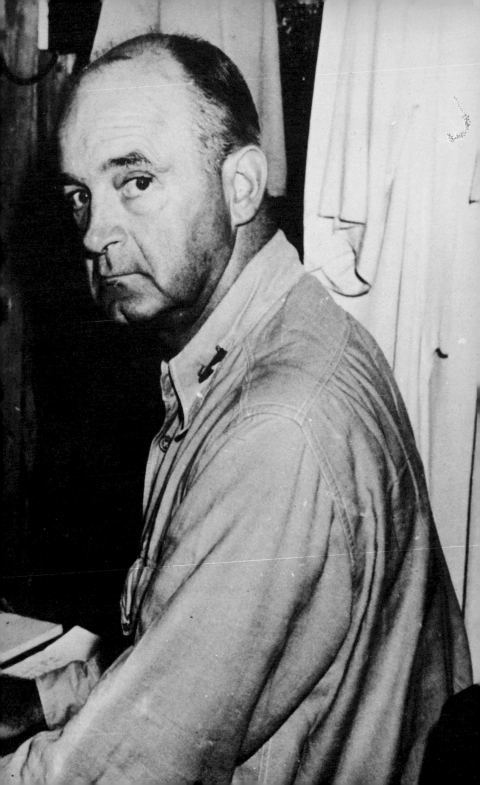

Marine commander but the suave admiral's hands were tied. Vandegrift would just have to go ahead and make his preparations as best he could. As a concession he would be allowed the 2nd Marines of the 2nd Division who would leave San Diego on 1st July.

Grimly Vandegrift and his staff set to work to accomplish as much as they could in the time available. The first problem to be faced was that no one seemed to know anything about Tulagi and Guadalcanal. From his headquarters at the Cecil Hotel in Wellington Vandegrift sent his Intelligence Officer, Lieutenant-Colonel Goettge, to Australia to interview missionaries, planters and Government officers who had recently left the Solomons. A great deal of information was accumulated, some of it useful but some considerably misleading as was to be discovered on Guadalcanal. There was neither the time for nor the means of checking facts. Goettge arranged for eight of the Solomons veterans to be commissioned so that they could accompany the marines as guides upon the expedition, and returned to General Vandegrift.

Nothing seemed to be happening in an orderly manner. In Vandegrift's own words: 'there was no time for a deliberate planning phase, and in many instances irrevocable decisions had to be made even before the essential features of the Naval plan of operations could be ascertained.' Particularly worrying was the lack of detailed knowledge of the area to be invaded. Two Marine officers were sent on a B-17 reconnaissance flight over Guadalcanal. Their aircraft was attacked by Japanese floatplanes from Tulagi. The B-17 shot down two of the Zeros and reached Port Moresby in safety, but the observers had seen little of Guadalcanal. As July progressed it became apparent that Operation Watchtower could not be

launched on 1st August. Accordingly on 10th June the date of the assault was postponed to 7th August.

The chain of command was also being hammered out. From Noumea Ghormley was to be in charge of strategy, reporting to Nimitz. Acting for Ghormley on the spot would be Vice-Admiral Fletcher. Immediately below Fletcher was Rear-Admiral Kelly Turner who was the commander of the amphibious force. Turner's second-in-command was Rear-Admiral V A C Crutchley, RN, a red-bearded hero of the First World War. The latter's covering force consisted of both US and Australian vessels. In charge of all land-based aircraft was Vice-Admiral John S McCain, Commander, Aircraft, South Pacific, who had been responsible for ordering the construction of the airfield at Espiritu Santo.

In New Zealand marines sweated desperately to prepare for the landings. Supplies were unloaded and sorted in conditions so unpleasant that New Zealand dock workers refused to work in them. Police cleared the dockers from the wharves and the marines worked in eight-hour shifts loading and unloading their own supplies.

The day of Operation Watchtower approached, anticipated with growing apprehension by those responsible for its planning. MacArthur and Ghormley recommended a further postponement. King refused to grant it. Later the admiral was to comment with considerable understatement: 'Because of the urgency of seizing and occupying Guadalcanal, planning was not up to the usual standard.'

Amid all the confusion Vandegrift was occupied with planning the first US amphibious landing in time of war since 1898. The state of the shoreline on which his marines were to land remained largely unknown, and he was not assisted when specially commissioned photographic maps of Guadalcanal were mislaid in a New Zealand warehouse. Neither was the estimate of Japanese forces any more

Major-General Alexander A Vandegrift, who led the assault on Guadalcanal

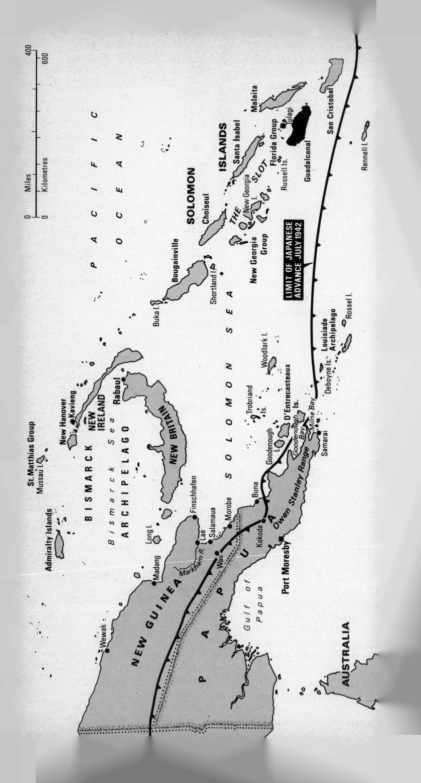

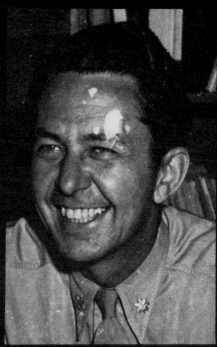

Brigadier-General William H Rupertus   **Lieutenant-Colonel Harold E Rosecrans**

Rear-Admiral Kelly Turner (left) plans the operation with General Vandegrift

precise. It was supposed that some 5,000 enemy troops occupied the area to be assaulted, a considerable over-estimate as it turned out.

Throughout the frenetic month of July Vandegrift and his staff doggedly continued to draw up plans. It was confirmed that there would be two thrusts – one at Guadalcanal and the other directed at Tulagi and the neighbouring islands of Gavatu, Tanambogo and the Floridas. It was hoped that the landing force on Guadalcanal (Group X-ray) would encounter relatively muted opposition. On Tulagi, however, the enemy would have to stand and fight, and heavy casualties could be expected. Accordingly Vandegrift allocated what he considered his best-trained forces to the Tulagi operation. Under the over-all command of Brigadier-General William H Rupertus were to be the 1st Marine Raider Battalion and its leader Lieutenant-Colonel Merritt A Edson, the 1st Parachute Battalion of Major Robert H Williams, and Lieutenant-Colonel Harold E Rosecrans' 2nd Battalion of the 5th Marines. The Guadalcanal landing would be commanded by Vandegrift himself, leading the remainder of the 1st Marine Division and any special and service troops.

The entire force would be convoyed to the Solomons in what was in effect the greater part of the US Navy in the Pacific at that time: the aircraft carriers *Saratoga*, *Enterprise* and *Wasp*, the battleship *North Carolina*, and a number of cruisers and destroyers to escort the transports. Altogether 959 officers and 18,156 enlisted men would be transported in this expeditionary force.

Owing to the shortage of landing craft it would not be possible to launch simultaneous attacks on Tulagi and Guadalcanal. A careful timetable had to be prepared. At Tulagi, Edson's Raiders would go ashore on the south side, followed by the 2nd Battalion of the 5th Marines. They would fight their way inland and then strike to the east. The Parachute Battalion would wade ashore at the twin islands of Gavatu and Tanambogo and there would be an additional precautionary sweep along that shoreline of the Floridas closest to Tulagi.

The landing at Guadalcanal would take place to the east of the Lunga area, where it was possible that the Japanese had set up defensive positions. The 5th Marines, with the exception of the 2nd Battalion which would be on Tulagi, would go ashore and establish a beachhead two battalions abreast. The 1st Marines would join them and it should be possible to set up a suitable situation from which an attack to the west could follow.

While he was struggling to co-ordinate his plan of campaign Vandegrift was also endeavouring to solve all the other problems presented by attempting to gather together a large amphibious invasion force at short notice. Conditions at the docks continued to be chaotic. Amid the pouring rain of a New Zealand winter marines struggled to unload, sort and reload stores, working against the clock. Morale was not high. One civilian transport, the *Ericsson*, hired to bring Marines from the USA to New Zealand was the subject of particular obloquy. It had served food of a very low standard throughout the voyage, resulting in an average weight-loss of sixteen to twenty pounds among the men on board.

In an effort to save time Vandegrift ordered his units 'reduce their equipment and supplies to those items that are actually required to live and fight.' The ammunition allowance was reduced by fifty per cent. When the task force left New Zealand almost half the original supplies had been left behind, but the ships sailed as ordered at 0900 hours on 22nd July.

Ghormley ordered all vessels in the expedition to rendezvous at 1400 hours on 26th July. At that time Turner's Task Force 62 joined Fletcher's Task Force 61 near the island of Koro some 367 miles south

General Henry H Arnold

Vice-Admiral John S McCain

Rear-Admiral V A C Crutchley

Vice-Admiral Robert L Ghormley

of Fiji. A meeting of the commanders of the expedition was held on board the *Saratoga*. Ghormley was too busy to attend and was represented by Admiral Daniel J Callaghan. The meeting was not an inspiring one, serving as it did to emphasise the gaps in planning, lack of sympathy between Marshall and King of the Joint Chiefs of Staff, and the cumbersome and almost unworkable chain of command which had been forged for the operation.

At the meeting Fletcher made it plain that he saw his function as being leader of a hit-and-run operation, landing men and supplies and leaving as soon as possible. This view distressed Vandegrift who had counted on air and sea support for at least four days after the initial landing. It transpired that Ghormley had not supplied a 'Letter of Instruction' to Fletcher, who was pessimistic about the chances of success of Operation Watchtower. The fact that Rear-Admiral McCain, in charge of shore-based aircraft, worked direct to Ghormley and not to Turner also caused some confusion. Vandegrift received a further blow when he was informed that he would not be receiving the 2nd Marines as they were being diverted to occupy Ndeni in the

The hasty preparations. Amphibian tractors are loaded in New Zealand

Santa Cruz group among the Eastern Solomons. This last order was later rescinded.

Following this confused and inconclusive gathering, rehearsals of the projected landings which took place between 28th and 31st July did little to lift the general gloom. The coral beaches of Koro proved almost unassailable while the strictly imposed radio silence made it impossible to co-ordinate air and troop movements. Watching the shambles Vandegrift fretted to get away; precious time was being wasted.

The vessels regrouped and began their journey to the Solomons. So far little had gone right with the expedition. For the voyage from Fiji to Guadalcanal there was a reversal of fortune. The armada steamed across the sea without being spotted by the Japanese. At 0200 the island of Savo was sighted and then Cape Esperance. At daylight the cruisers began a bombardment of the shores of Guadalcanal and Tulagi, while carrier-based aircraft sank Japanese float planes at their moorings.

Red Beach
and after

the transports had reached their objectives some 9,000 yards off the beaches chosen for the landing operations. Men began to descend the cargo-net gangways to the Higgins boats waiting below. Everything proceeded calmly and efficiently, causing more than one observer to remark that this looked more like an exercise than the real thing.

In order to protect the left flank of the force landing at Tulagi, B Company of the 1st Battalion, 2nd Marine Regiment under Captain Edgar J Crane went ashore at the Florida Islands, thus laying claim to being the first American troops to land on enemy-held territory in the Second World War. Haleta village, their objective, was empty and so was Halavo the next village they came to. By noon Crane and his men regrouped on the beach. The Japanese had withdrawn from the Floridas.

The Tulagi landing took place as scheduled at 0800 on Blue Beach on the western shore a little more than a mile from the north-west tip of the island. There was no opposition from the Japanese on the beach, which was perhaps just as well because none of the landing-craft could negotiate the coral outcrops and the Raiders and marines had to wade ashore from as far as one hundred yards out. Edson's Raiders were first ashore, although their commander, held up by a faulty engine on his landing craft, did not catch up with his troops until they had pressed some way inland.

At 0614 on 7th August, the three cruisers and four destroyers of the Guadalcanal Fire Support Group began to bombard selected targets between Kukum and Koli Point along the north coast of the island. Two minutes later the single cruiser and two destroyers of the Tulagi Fire Support Group began firing at the shore of Tulagi. Eighty-five dive-bombers and fighters from the aircraft carriers now lurking seventy-five miles south-west of Guadalcanal, attacked Tulagi and Guadalcanal, destroying eighteen seaplanes at their moorings and encountering only spasmodic anti-aircraft fire.

By 0651, moving over a calm sea,

The Japanese on Tulagi fought heroically from their fox-holes and caves, but seemed aware from the outset of the impossibility of their situation. Their last radio message out at 0810 was 'Enemy troop strength is overwhelming. We will defend to the last man.' This proved to be almost literally true. Of the Japanese defenders on Tulagi, 200 were killed, about forty escaped by swimming to

Left: Marines climb down the side of a transport into an assault landing-craft. The first American landing of the war is under way. *Above:* Marines come ashore at Tulagi. *Below:* Tanambogo Island after the air bombardment

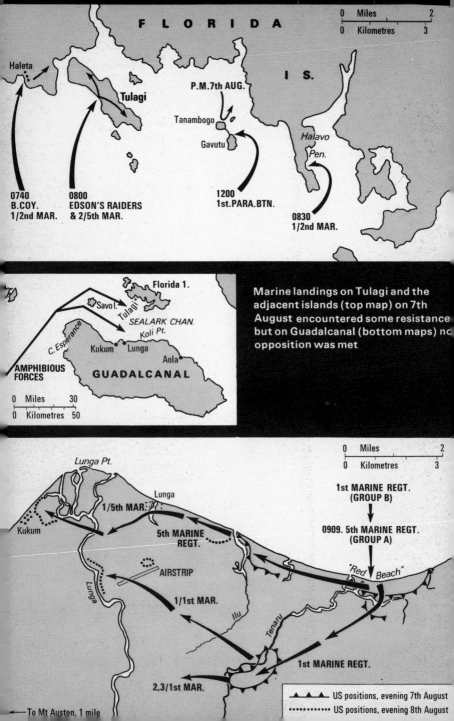

FLORIDA

0   Miles   2
0   Kilometres   3

Haleta

Tulagi

P.M.7th AUG.

Tanambogo

Gavutu

I S.

Halavo Pen.

0740
B.COY.
1/2nd MAR.

0800
EDSON'S RAIDERS
& 2/5th MAR.

1200
1st.PARA.BTN.

0830
1/2nd MAR.

Florida I.

Savo I.

Tulagi

SEALARK CHAN.

Koli Pt.

C. Esperance

Kukum   Lunga

Aola

**AMPHIBIOUS
FORCES**

GUADALCANAL

0   Miles   30
0   Kilometres   50

Marine landings on Tulagi and the
adjacent islands (top map) on 7th
August encountered some resistance
but on Guadalcanal (bottom maps) no
opposition was met

Lunga Pt.

Lunga

1/5th MAR.

Kukum

**5th MARINE
REGT.**

AIRSTRIP

Lunga

1/1st MAR.

Ilu

Tenaru

**1st MARINE REGT.
(GROUP B)**

**0909. 5th MARINE REGT.
(GROUP A)**

"Red   Beach"

1st MARINE REGT.

2,3/1st MAR.

0   Miles   2
0   Kilometres   3

▲▲▲ US positions, evening 7th August
•••••••• US positions, evening 8th August

◄— To Mt Austen, 1 mile

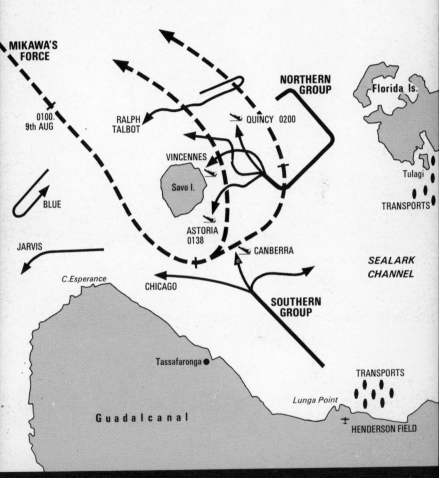

The Battle of Savo Island, 8/9th August 1942

the Floridas and three surrendered. The Americans realised that it was almost impossible to drive the Japanese out of their positions with small-arms fire and relied upon the use of grenades and explosives to bomb them out.

By late afternoon the Japanese had been driven back to a position in the south-eastern corner of the island. US radio communications had worsened as the day drew on but Edson managed to deliver a message to the effect that he could not take the island on that first day. He received permission to establish a line facing the cornered Japanese. Five Raider companies and G Company of the 5th Marines comprised this force. Among the Americans were two Britons, D C Horton and Henry Josselyn, former Administrative Officers in the

Left and below: The landing on Guadalcanal met with no opposition and the Marines quickly established their beachhead

Solomons and now sub-lieutenants in the Royal Australian Navy attached to the invading force. Horton and Josselyn had gone ashore with the sfirt wave of assault troops. Both were to receive the Silver Star for their work on Tulagi.

During the night of 7th–8th August the Japanese made a number of determined attempts to break out of their position. Some of them even reached the former Residency, now being used as a command post, but none of them succeeded in forcing their way free. On the morning of 8th August Edson was joined by F and E Companies of the 5th Marine Regiment. The marines had been clearing the Japanese out of north-west Tulagi. With his augmented force Edson attacked and overcame the remaining Japanese. By mid-afternoon on 8th August Tulagi had been successfully occupied. Thirty-six Americans had been killed and fifty-four wounded.

The Japanese on the tiny adjoining islands of Gavutu and Tanambogo

Above: Chaos on Red Beach as mounds of supplies build up — one result of hurried operational planning. *Below:* Marines move inland

put up as spirited a resistance as their brothers-in-arms on Tulagi. On 7th August at 1145 hours the vessels of the Tulagi Fire Support Group shelled Gavatu while the men of the 1st Parachute Battalion approached in their landing craft. The first troops landed successfully but succeeding waves were cut down by withering small-arms fire coming from the defenders. The men of the Parachute Battalion advanced inland to lay siege to the small hill occupied by the Japanese. The Japanese defended grimly, aided by fire support from their colleagues on Tanambogo, and it was not until 1800 hours that the US troops took the hill. They were still mopping up the following day.

Tanambogo is connected to Gavatu by a concrete causeway, but the US forces could not at first storm the island either by land or sea. Neither bombing raids nor naval artillery could subdue the Japanese entrenched in this last-ditch stand. As an emergency measure B Company of the 2nd Marines were withdrawn from the Floridas and flung into action in a landing on the north coast of Tanambogo. The attack was beaten off bloodily. On 8th August at 1130 hours the 2nd Marines and two light tanks made a simultaneous attack from the beach and the causeway. The Japanese fought courageously – it seemed that this was the only way they knew how to fight – but early evening Tanambogo was in the hands of the Marines. On Gavatu and Tanambogo about 500 Japanese and 108 Americans had been slaughtered.

While Tulagi and the neighbouring islands had been the scene of vicious fighting, the landings on Guadalcanal had taken place calmly and without any show of resistance. After the initial bombardment the Japanese – some 600 fighting men and 1,400 labourers – had fled inland in some confusion, leaving the way clear for the Marines to land at Red Beach. Reconnaissance planes from the cruiser *Astoria* confirmed the absence of enemy troops. At 0909 Colonel LeRoy P Hunt led Combat Group 'A' ashore at Red Beach. His men spread out to cover a front of 2,000 yards. The invasion of Guadalcanal had begun.

The First Marines Combat Group 'B', were the next to land. Led by Colonel Clifton B Cates, like Hunt a veteran of the First World War, the marines advanced past Group 'A' (5th Marines) and began to advance on Mount Austen. During the preparations for the attack this mountain had been called 'Grassy Knoll', and it had been believed to be about two miles inland. The information had been faulty. Mount Austen is some four miles inland, as the Marines of Combat Group 'B' soon became only too well aware.

At the beachhead things went well for the first three hours. Troops were ferried ashore swiftly and without complications. The lack of opposition proved something of an anti-climax to some of the troops, especially as the firing from Tulagi indicated that the men under Rupertus' command were in the thick of the fighting. Vandegrift, however, was delighted by the smoothness of the operation so far. It was true that reports were coming through that Cates and the 1st Marines had slowed down considerably, but at least his men were getting ashore in one piece.

The situation was not nearly so satisfactory when it came to the stores and supplies. Not enough men had been made available to unload these and carry them forward from Red Beach. As the day wore on the mounds of supplies grew larger and larger as more landing craft nosed ashore with boxes. The combat troops, although they had not been in action could not be detached for such duty while there was a chance that the Japanese would attack the beachhead. At one time one hundred boats had landed their supplies on the shore and another fifty were waiting their turn to approach the beach.

A message went to Vandegrift informing him that another 500 men were needed for the unloading. All that could be offered were fifteen from each cargo ship. By late evening the Commander of the shore party was forced to report that the situation was out of hand, and a halt was called to supplies coming from the ships. The official report laid the blame for the chaos on 'a total lack of conception of the number of labour troops required to unload boats and move material off the beach, failure to extend the beach limits earlier in the operation, and, to some extent, lack of control of troops on and in the immediate vicinity of the beach . . .'

The lack of organisation over the supply situation and the faulty intelligence leading to the failure of Cates and his 1st Marines to reach Mount Austen were Vandegrift's two major worries. Otherwise everything had gone well with the Guadalcanal landing. Vandegrift concentrated on trying to keep to his original schedule. At 1400 he ordered the 1st Battalion of the 5th Marines to advance westwards to Alligator Creek and dig in for the night. Two hours later General Vandegrift came ashore and set up his command post. By this time there had been two Japanese air strikes. The first had occurred at 1320. Rear-Admiral Sadayoshi Yamada, in command of the Japanese 25th Air Flotilla, sent twenty-four aircraft to bomb Tulagi. Warning of the attack had been sent by one of the ubiquitous coastwatchers and the Americans were prepared. Twelve Japanese aircraft were shot down by Wildcats based on the carrier *Saratoga*, but the destroyer *Mugford* was hit and twenty-two men killed. At 1500 hours there was an attack by ten Aichi 99 dive bombers and then the Japanese were seen no more that day. Six US float planes, three from the *Astoria* and three from the *Quincy* occupied the

skies above Guadalcanal, utilised for smoke laying to mark the extremities of the landing beaches and as spotter aircraft for the Marine artillery.

By early evening the advance of Cates and his marines had slowed almost to a halt, affected by the heat and undergrowth. Vandegrift realised that there would be no chance of reaching Mount Austen that day. Accordingly he changed his plans, issuing fresh orders from his command post. The marines were to dig in for the night. On the following morning

the 1st Marines would head westwards towards the Lunga, forgetting about Mount Austen, and occupy the airstrip from the south. The 5th Marines were also to advance on the Lunga and then continue to Kukum.

The night of the 7th-8th of August was a noisy one, but only because a great many nervous marines fired at shadows. There was no Japanese attack. The following morning, Saturday 8th August at 0930 1st Battalion of the 5th Marines, supported by the 1st Tank Battalion, crossed the mouth of Alligator Creek. This was in fact

The Mitsubishi G4M (code name 'Betty'). The Japanese navy's principal wartime bomber. But the demands of its strike and support role had to be paid for in lack of adequate defensive armament. *Maximum speed:* 276mph. *Armament:* up to five 7.7mm machine guns and a 1,765 lb bomb-load. *Range:* 2,630 miles.

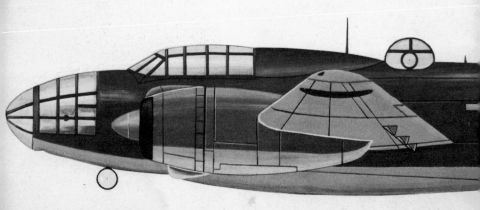

reached and passed the airfield, but the 2nd and 3rd Battalions, slowed down in their turn, were still south of the airstrip when the time came to dig in for the night.

The 5th Marines made satisfactory progress and also encountered individual Japanese troops who had been slow to retreat. A few prisoners were taken and it was ascertained from these that there was unlikely to be any immediate Japanese resistance. This caused Vandegrift to order the 5th Marines to regroup and advance more quickly on a less extended front. The regiment crossed the Lunga over the main bridge. Skirting the airfield to the north it advanced to Kukum, capturing large quantities of abandoned food and equipment.

Back at the beachhead the day had been less satisfactory for the Americans. Another force of Japanese aircraft, Betty bombers escorted by Zero fighters, had swept down from Rabaul. Jack Read, the coastwatcher on Bougainville relayed this information to Australia from whence it was transmitted to Fletcher and Turner off Guadalcanal. All transport vessels

the Ilu River, although more faulty intelligence caused the marines to believe it was the Tenaru, and it was by the last name that it continued to be known for some time. Acting on its instructions the 1st Battalion of the 1st Marines swung west away from Mount Austen and began its advance. Again this unit moved very slowly and made hard work of crossing a creek, while the 2nd and 3rd Battalions moved rather more rapidly through the jungle. The day was a long, hot one. At the end of it the 1st Battalion of the 1st Marines had

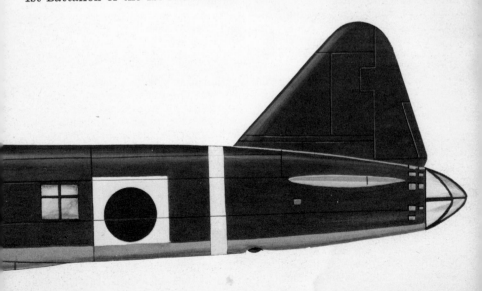

George F Elliott on fire after the
Japanese attack

and cargo ships stopped unloading and
put to sea as Wildcats from the
Saratoga took off and maintained a
position over Savo island. The attacking Japanese aircraft eluded the
Wildcats but ran into heavy anti-
aircraft fire which repulsed the low-
flying torpedo bombers. Some got
through, however. One Betty crashed
on to the deck of the transport *George
F Elliott*, exploding and setting fire to
the ship. The destroyer *Jarvis* was
also put out of action.

The Americans had cause to be
proud of the efficacy of their Wildcat
pilots and their anti-aircraft gunners,
but by 8th August Fletcher was a
very worried man. His fighter
strength had been whittled down from
99 to 78 aircraft and supplies of fuel
were dangerously low. Fletcher decided that he could not afford to
hazard Task Force 61 by allowing it
to remain off the shores of Guadalcanal. At 1807 on 8th August he
contacted Ghormley and made a
strong case for withdrawing his

carriers. Ghormley was reluctant to
grant such a request but felt that he
was too far from the scene of operations to deny a demand couched in
such urgent terms. The request was
granted. It was one of the most
controversial decisions made during
the whole Guadalcanal campaign.
Fletcher had enough fuel for several
more days, the Japanese air attacks
had been beaten off and most of his
ships were undamaged. In addition,
half the supplies had yet to be unloaded.

Ghormley's decision was relayed to
Turner. The latter, renowned for his
colourful bursts of profanity, was
remarkably restrained, although later
he was to refer bitterly to this 'desertion of the vital parts of the force'.
Turner summoned Vandegrift and
Rear-Admiral Crutchley to his flagship
the *McCawley*, and informed them that
Fletcher was leaving and taking with
him their air support and a considerable proportion of their supplies.
With some understatement Vandegrift called the move 'most alarming'.
Turner agreed briefly and then went
into points of detail. Not all the

Above: USS Astoria. Below: USS Vincennes

The Mitsubishi A6M Zero came as a complete surprise to the Allies. Convinced that Japanese aircraft were no more than inferior copies of their western counterparts, they were suddenly faced with a superlative fighter aircraft – fast, agile, with a high rate of climb, a good range and a heavy armament. And so at the beginning of the Pacific and South East Asian campaigns the Zero was the prime factor in the skies, and can be said to have had a major influence on Japanese strategic thinking as a result pilots soon learnt to exploit these and so hold the Zeros. These two faults were inadequate protection for pilot and fuel, and a relatively light construction, which meant that the Zero could not take much damage. *Engine:* Nakajima Sakae 21 radial, 1,130 hp. *Armament:* Two 20mm cannon and two 7.7mm machine guns plus up to 264 pounds of bombs. *Maximum speed:* 351 mph at 19,685 feet. *Climb rate:* 4,500 feet per minute. *Ceiling:* 35,100 feet. *Range:* 1,000 miles. *Weight loaded:* 6,047 pounds. *Span:* 36 feet 1 inch. *Length:* 29 feet 8¾ inches

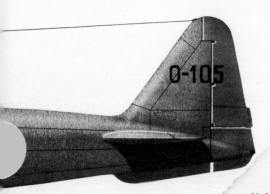

Nakajima A6M2-N (Allied code name 'Rufe'). *Engine:* Nakajima Sakae 950hp at take off. *Armament:* Two 7.7mm Type 97 machine guns, and two 20mm Type 99 Model 1 Mark 3 cannon and two 132 lbs bombs. *Speed:* 270.5mph at 16,405 feet. *Climb rate:* 16,405 feet in 6 minutes 43 seconds. *Ceiling:* 32,810 feet. *Range:* 714 miles. *Weight empty:* 4,235 lbs. *Weight loaded:* 5,423 lbs. *Span:* 39 feet 4½ inches. *Length:* 33 feet 1⅝ inches

American cruisers involved in the Battle of Savo island, 8/9th August 1942:
Above: USS Quincy. Below: USS Chicago

vessels were to be removed. Crutchley was to be left in command of the mixed Australian and US cruiser group which consisted of *Australia, Canberra, Chicago, Vincennes, Astoria, Quincy* and six destroyers.

While a bitter meeting was taking place on the *McCawley*, a Japanese naval force was approaching Guadalcanal with orders to attack and destroy the US transports at anchor off the island. This force was under the command of Vice-Admiral Mikawa, the Commander-in-Chief of the Eighth Fleet, and was made up of five heavy and two light cruisers and a destroyer. On 8th August as the ships were making their way down the coast of Bougainville they had been spotted by two Australian reconnaissance planes. The pilots either delivered incorrect reports or the reports were garbled upon reception, because the message was not received by Admiral Turner until 1800 hours. Turner assumed that the Japanese force was heading for Gizo but passed the report on to Crutchley as a routine matter.

Meanwhile Mikawa, leading the expeditionary force in *Chokai*, sailed down 'the Slot' between the two chains of Solomon Islands and approached Savo without being seen. Crutchley had left no battle plan with his vessels while he conferred with Turner and Vandegrift. Two destroyers equipped with radar, the *Blue* and the *Ralph Talbot* were stationed on either side of the channel north-west of the island of Savo. Between Savo and Cape Esperance the waters were being patrolled by the cruisers *Australia, Canberra* and *Chicago*, and the destroyers *Bagley* and *Patterson*. Further patrol activity was being undertaken between Savo and the Floridas by the cruisers *Vincennes, Astoria* and *Quincy*, and the destroyers *Helm* and *Wilson*. Two other cruisers and a number of destroyers supervised the transports.

Mikawa sailed cautiously towards Savo as night fell, expecting at any moment to be observed. His luck held. At midnight a number of seaplanes left his cruisers and headed for the American and Australian vessels. They were heard by the Americans who reported unidentified aircraft overhead. Still the Japanese vessels were not seen. At 0145 on the 9th August one aircraft from the *Chokai* dropped flares over the American transports. At the same time the Japanese ships sailed between the *Blue* and the *Ralph Talbot* under the cover of darkness. Neither radar nor look-outs reported the intruders, although the *Blue* in particular was very close to the enemy vessels slipping past through the channel.

Once he was past the entrance Mikawa signalled for speed to be increased to thirty knots. Then his vessels opened fire and launched torpedoes at the *Canberra* and *Chicago*. The US Navy was about to suffer one of its most disastrous defeats. The *Canberra* was destroyed, its hulk to be sunk the following morning by US destroyers. The *Chicago* was crippled, its bows ripped off. Acting with precision Mikawa's force now split up, four vessels heading north-east and three going due north. At 0145 Japanese vessels bore down on *Astoria, Quincy* and *Vincennes*. The ships in Mikawa's command picked out the American vessels in their searchlights and unleased a dreadful onslaught of 8-inch shells and torpedoes. The *Astoria* fought back but was gutted by fire, sinking the following day. The *Quincy* went down at 0235. Fifteen minutes later the *Vincennes* sank. Mikawa had achieved the most astounding naval victory. The US transports lay defenceless before him. Had Mikawa gone forward and destroyed them it is possible that the course of the Guadalcanal campaign and even the Pacific war might have been altered, but the admiral did not do so. There were a number of reasons for his caution. One shell from the *Astoria* had destroyed the control room of *Chokai*, his vessels had been

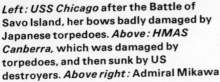

Left: USS Chicago after the Battle of Savo Island, her bows badly damaged by Japanese torpedoes. *Above: HMAS Canberra,* which was damaged by torpedoes, and then sunk by US destroyers. *Above right:* Admiral Mikawa

slow to regroup, there was the possibility that aircraft from the carriers of Task Force 61 would destroy his force. Admiral Mikawa felt that all things considered he had done enough. At 0223 he signalled to his vessels to withdraw. At the entrance to the channel off Savo there was a brief engagement with *Ralph Talbot* in a heavy rainstorm and the American vessel was damaged before the Japanese had passed out of range.

Mikawa sailed back to Rabaul and the congratulations of his countrymen. There was a quiet word of reproof from his superior Admiral Yamamoto, the Commander-in-Chief Combined Fleet, for not having attacked the transports as well, but the Japanese as a whole treated the Battle of Savo Island as the resounding victory it had been. Even the fact that Mikawa lost one ship, *Kako,* to an

American submarine on the return journey did not detract from his efforts.

For the first hours of daylight on 9th August rescue craft were busy picking up survivors from the sea off Guadalcanal. In five hours some 700 men were ferried ashore. The stories of these survivors brought home to the marines on the island the full magnitude of the Japanese victory during the hours of darkness. In an effort to avoid depressing the public at home King did not release details of the debacle off Ironbottom Sound, as it came to be called, for some weeks. When the people at home realised the full extent of the naval defeat suffered by the vessels under Crutchley's command there was a virulent press campaign against the unfortunate Englishman.

The Savo disaster confirmed Fletcher in his desire to remove his task force from the danger area. The rest of the daylight hours of 9th August were spent in preparations for departure. By sundown Task Force 61 had sailed away from Guadalcanal, leaving the marines on their own.

Left: The Japanese cruiser *Chokai,* Mikawa's flagship at Savo Island. *Above:* Transports steam out of Ironbottom Sound on 10th August 1942, after Admiral Fletcher had decided to withdraw Task Force 61. *Below: USS Bagley*

Counterattack

immediate project was to make the vital airfield operational. Until that was accomplished he would throw a defensive wall around it. This line of defence extended from the Lunga area to the Ilu River. At the same time his marines had to be on the alert for a Japanese sea-based attack. It was a case of digging in, and that was exactly what the marines did. A line of fortified fox-holes ran round the perimeter of the area to be held. Thirty-calibre and fifty-calibre machine guns were installed, backed by 37mm guns. 90mm AA guns were sited around the airfield and Vandegrift ordered that his tanks were to be in constant readiness for combat.

.Fortunately the August weather, although oppressive, was fine. It was not until later that the rains came. In the meantime there were the malaria-bearing mosquitoes and such tropical afflictions as jungle-rot to be contended with. There were also the low-level Japanese bombing raids and the spasmodic shelling from enemy surface craft and submarines off the coast of Guadalcanal.

Vandegrift sent out probing patrols. It became plain that the Japanese had retreated to the west and were camping on the banks of the Matanikau River near Kukum. Any American patrols venturing across this river were driven back by accurate small-arms fire, sometimes with loss of life. It was near the Matanikau that Vandegrift lost his intelligence officer, Lieutenant-Colonel Goettge, and over twenty men of a patrol sent to investigate a report from a prisoner that Japanese in the area were waiting to surrender. The patrol was ambushed and only three men escaped alive.

On Guadalcanal Vandegrift took stock of his situation. The prospect was not an encouraging one. The Americans had lost control of the seas around the Solomons. The nearest source of air support was Espiritu Santo in the New Hebrides. There had not been time to unload half the supplies before Task Force 61 steamed away. Already there were grave shortages of food and materials. Morale among the troops, suffering from the heat and humidity and disillusioned by what they regarded as the desertion of the navy, was not high.

Vandegrift decided that he was in no position to attack. The schedule that he drew up heavily emphasised defence. The most important and

Many of the marines on Guadalcanal felt that they had been left to die, comparing their situation with that of the men left on Bataan. Their feeling of isolation was lessened

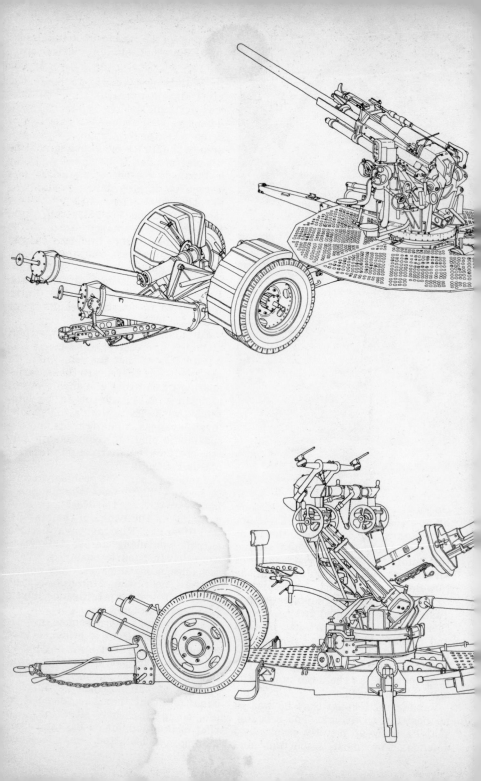

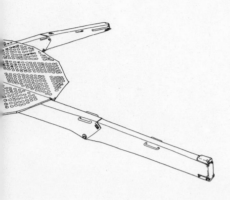

US 90mm Anti-Aircraft gun. *Calibre:*
90mm. *Weight of shell:* 23 lbs (HE and
AP). *Muzzle velocity:* 2,700 feet per
second. *Vertical range:* 30,000 feet.
Rate of fire: 28 rounds per minute
maximum, 18 normal. *Weight:* 32,300 lbs.
Maximum travelling speed: 20mph

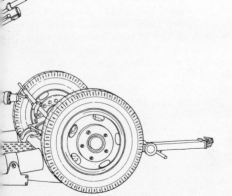

US 37mm Anti-Aircraft gun. *Calibre:*
37mm. *Weight of shell:* 1.34 lbs HE and
1.9 lbs AP. *Muzzle velocity:* 2,600 feet
per second. *Vertical range:* 6,200 feet.
Horizontal range: 8,775 feet.
Elevation: −5° to +90°. *Traverse:* 360°.
Rate of fire: 120 rounds per minute.
Weight: 5,300 to 6,100 pounds.
Maximum travelling speed: 50mph

slightly on 14th August when three destroyer transports *Little, McKean* and *Gregory* ran the gauntlet of enemy aircraft and surface vessels to land fuel, ammunition and other supplies.

On 17th August, worried by the proximity of the Japanese on the west bank of the Matanikau, Vandegrift set in motion a minor operation to protect his lines by driving the enemy back. The venture, a three-pronged one, was successful but Vandegrift was not reassured by the number of details which went wrong. Three companies were briefed to attack the Japanese. One, under the command of Captain Lyman D Spurlock, was to make its way inland for half a mile, cross the river and then attack in the direction of the sea, that is in the direction from which it had advanced. Covering fire would be provided from the east bank of the river by a company under Captain William L Hawkins who was later to cross the river himself if possible. Captain Bert W Hardy Jr would take a third company by boat

two miles west of the river, come ashore at Kokumbona and advance to the east.

The operation took place on 19th August, two days after it had been planned and became the first substantial encounter between the two forces on Guadalcanal. Detailed to give covering fire, Hawkins found that his company was itself pinned down by Japanese machine gunners on the far side of the Matanikau. Nevertheless Spurlock took his company forward, with some losses, as far as Matanikau village. Radio communications, as happened too often, broke down and the third company under Hardy was considerably delayed because their small boat had been shelled by a Japanese submarine while hugging the coast.

Spurlock's advance guard was already under fire. He decided not to break off contact with the enemy and gave the order to go forward. The Japanese regrouped and launched a bayonet charge, one of the famed

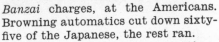

Left: A Marine patrol crosses the Lunga River on a mission towards the Matanikau River. *Above:* Colonel Goettge

Banzai charges, at the Americans. Browning automatics cut down sixty-five of the Japanese, the rest ran.

Hardy's company, in the meantime, having avoided the submarine then ran into two Japanese destroyers but managed to escape and complete a delayed landing near the enemy-occupied village of Kokumbona. After a brief engagement the Japanese fled into the jungle. The Americans had secured their lines and made their beachhead a little safer.

Vandegrift was satisfied with this his first limited land action, but was far from happy with the situation as a whole. He did not have enough men or supplies to advance and he had his doubts about the ability of his men to repulse a sustained attack from superior Japanese forces, an opinion shared by Ghormley when he advised King that the Japanese might drive the marines back into the sea unless reinforcements were sent. There was a growing feeling among top military personnel in Washington that while the amphibious landing in the Solomons had been successful, there had not been nearly enough planning or preparation for the war of attrition which seemed to be approaching. Few members of the Joint Chiefs of Staff would have agreed with President Roosevelt's message to Joseph Stalin on 19th August: 'We have gained a toe hold in the South West Pacific from which the Japanese will find it very difficult to dislodge us ... and we are going to maintain hard pressure on the enemy.'

Fortunately for the Allied cause, the Japanese military command seemed almost as confused over the Guadalcanal campaign as the Americans. It was at first believed in Tokyo that the Americans would soon abandon this 'insignificant' island. When it became plain that Vandegrift was digging in, plans were hastily made to dislodge him. Lieutenant-General Haruyoshi Hyakutake and the Seventeenth Army were ordered to retake Guadalcanal and Tulagi before turning to the more

important task of capturing Port Moresby. There were 50,000 men in Hyakutake's force but they were not all in one place. The 2nd Division was in Java and the Philippines, other units were in New Guinea, Manchuria, the Dutch East Indies and Guam. The general was not unduly perturbed by his lack of strength. One crack fighting unit should be enough to drive the Americans from the Solomons. Colonel Kiyanao Ichiki and the 28th Infantry from Guam should be capable of performing the task before the rest of the Seventeenth Army regrouped and stormed New Guinea.

Colonel Ichiki was a brave and experienced officer who had fought with distinction in China. Events proved him to be rash and impetuous but in August 1942 he must have seemed the ideal man to retake Guadalcanal. His orders were to 'quickly recapture and maintain the airfields at Guadalcanal. If this is not possible, this detachment will occupy a part of Guadalcanal and await the arrival of troops in its rear.' Ichiki was directed to take a spearhead of 900 soldiers on six destroyers and land at Taivu Point, some twenty miles from the Americans soon after midnight on 18th August. The remaining 2,500 men of his detachment would follow close behind, certainly within seven days.

On Guadalcanal General Vandegrift continued to send out patrols. He was aided in this by the fact that on 14th August a bearded and rather tattered young Englishman had reported to the American headquarters, having made his way through the Japanese lines with twenty natives carrying presents of fresh fruit! This had been Martin Clemens, coastwatcher and former district officer. Vandegrift accepted the Englishman's offer of help gratefully. Intelligence reports of Japanese shipping movements had been forwarded to him, while Clemens himself confirmed that there had been

a build-up of Japanese forces to the east. Clemens and his scouts, among them Sergeant-Major Jacob Vouza, a retired policeman who had come forward eagerly to offer his services upon the outbreak of hostilities in the Solomons, conducted a number of patrols in co-operation with the marines.

Around midnight on 18th August sentries on the Guadalcanal beach heard the wash of vessels passing. They were the destroyers of Ichiki's spearhead about to land the soldiers twenty-two miles east of the American beachhead. The following morning Sergeant-Major Vouza was sent out in charge of a small patrol to see what could be discovered. That same morning Captain Charles Brush, accompanied by four Solomon Islands policemen and eighty marines of Able Company, 1st Marines, headed east towards Koli Point on a similar searching venture. At noon some Japanese soldiers were seen. It transpired that they were members of Ichiki's force. Brush took up position in front of the unsuspecting Japanese, and sent his executive officer, Lieutenant Joseph Jachym to the right to take up position to the left of the enemy and behind them. Both groups of marines opened fire at the same time, killing thirty-one of thirty-four Japanese. Upon investigation of the dead it was discovered that they were army personnel, not the navy men who had previously been fighting the Americans on Guadalcanal. There was also a high proportion of officers among the dead. More important still, some of the officers carried accurate maps of the Tenaru area, emphasising the weak points of the marines' defence. (It was later discovered that Japanese on Mount Austen had kept the American lines under extremely close surveillance.)

It was clear that Japanese army forces had been landed and that their intelligence service was good. What was not so obvious was when they would attack and from which direction

Sergeant-Major Jacob Vouza. His scars were caused by Japanese bayonetting

Fighting on Guadalcanal was confined to the northern coastal strip

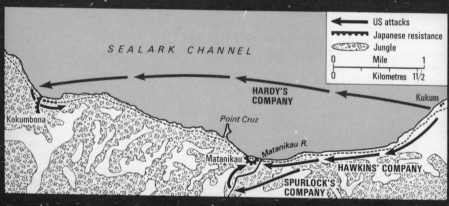

The attack on Matanikau, 19th August 1942

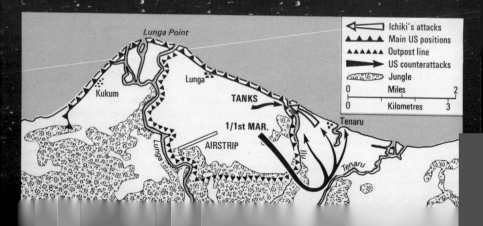

they would come. Vandegrift ordered all his force on to a state of constant alert.

While Captain Brush and Able Company had been wiping out the Japanese patrol Vouza had also made contact with the enemy. He had in fact been captured by them. His captors tied him to a tree and interrogated him, telling Vouza that he would be killed if he did not reveal the location of all the American troops in the area. Vouza remained silent. He was bayoneted in the face, neck and chest. His arm was slashed with a sword and he was left for dead. After the Japanese had gone Vouza managed to release himself and crawl back to the American lines, making a report about the Japanese strength before going to the hospital. For his heroism Vouza was awarded the Silver Star and the George Medal.

It was in the early morning of 21st August that Ichiki began his attack on the American line near the mouth of Alligator Creek on the Ilu River (still known as the Tenaru to the Americans.) Ichiki had decided that the 900 men he had with him would be sufficient for the task and that he need not wait for the 2,500 still to be transported to Guadalcanal. The time had come for Japan to counterattack.

At 0240 the attack came. Operation *Ka*, the Japanese attempt to retake Guadalcanal, was under way. Ichiki assembled his men in the jungle to the east of the river, opposite the sandbank. His mobile artillery opened fire on the Americans on the far side of the river and his *Nambu* light machine guns opened up. Then Ichiki led five hundred of his men in a *banzai* charge across the sandbank. The Americans opened fire with everything they had: machine guns, automatic rifles, mortars and grenades. Many Japanese were cut down while crossing the river. A few reached the far side and were held up by the American barbed wire and were slaughtered while trying to extricate themselves.

Those Japanese who were still alive fled back to the east side of the river.

At 0500 they tried again. This time Ichiki led his men round the sandbank at the mouth of the river, running through the surf pounding up from the sea. Cannons and mortars gave them a little covering fire. The object of their attack was the American beach position, less heavily fortified than the others. This was commanded by Lieutenant-Colonel Edwin A Pollock, in charge of 2nd Battalion, First Marines. Screams of 'Marine you die!' heralded the approach of the Japanese. Pollock's marksmen picked off the attackers one by one. Again Ichiki was forced to retreat, his command decimated.

Some of the Japanese remained, however; they could be heard moving in the jungle on the east side of the river erroneously believed to be the Tenaru. Colonel Gerald C Thomas, Divisional Operations Officer, urged Vandegrift to order an immediate advance. Hundreds of Japanese bodies lay on the sandbank and on both sides of the river. A swift attack could envelop the survivors and drive them into the sea. Vandegrift agreed. He came up to Cate's command post and issued the instruction. The reserve battalion, Cate's 1st Battalion, 1st Marines under Lieutenant-Colonel LB Creswell, was ordered to cross the river upstream, turn right and drive the Japanese down to the sea while Pollock's provided a withering hail of fire across the river. A platoon of light tanks would be brought up to help in the venture. Marine aircraft, too, could be used.

The operation succeeded. Creswell's Marines crossed the river and chased the Japanese from their foxholes. The airstrip, newly operational, provided aircraft for strafing operations. Pollock's artillery and automatic fire added to the carnage, while the tanks lumbering across the sandbank crushed bodies beneath their tracks until, in Vandegrift's words 'the rear of the tanks looked like meat grinders.'

The Battle of Tenaru: 'Hundreds of Japanese bodies lay on the sandbank'

By late afternoon the Battle of Tenaru (Ilu) was over. 800 Japanese had been killed, 15 taken prisoner. Many of the survivors died of their wounds in the jungle. The Americans lost 43 dead. Colonel Ichiki was was among the survivors who managed to reach Taivu. With him was his regimental flag. The colonel poured oil over the tattered rag, burned it and then shot himself.

The Battle of Tenaru was in many ways a turning point. Above all it destroyed the myth of Japanese supremacy. The Japanese were still obviously brave and determined fighters, even the wounded lying on the banks of the Tenaru continued to fight as long as they could hurl grenades or squeeze a trigger, but they were not the supermen of legend. They could be defeated. The Americans had proved this on the islands around Tulagi and confirmed it on the banks of the Ilu River. The superiority of Japanese military strategy was also proved to be largely illusory. Colonel Ichiki had blundered badly at the Battle of Tenaru. His head-on attack on the main American position had been disastrous. After his exploratory patrol had been almost wiped out a more cautious approach up-river through the jungle would have seemed called for. The answer probably lies in Ichiki's natural arrogance and the belief, shared at the time by his superiors in the Japanese High Command, that the Americans on Guadalcanal were in no shape to withstand a determined attack. Ichiki's supposition had been proven incorrect and the resultant boost for American morale at home and among the marines on Guadalcanal was incalculable.

Despite the local victory over Ichiki there was a great deal to be done before Vandegrift's position on Guadalcanal could be called secure. The Japanese would be more deter-

The US M3A1 General Stuart (nicknamed Honey) light tank was the first US tank to see service in the Second World War. A simple and sturdy design, it was well-armoured for its time and conditions of tactical operation, fast and adequately gunned. *Crew:* 4. *Weight:* 12.9 tons. *Armament:* one L6 37mm gun with 111 rounds and three Browning .3-inch machine guns with 7,000 rounds. *Maximum speed:* 36mph (road). *Range:* 60 miles. *Armour:* 2 inch lower front and turret front, $1\frac{1}{2}$ inches driver's front and turret sides and rear, 1 inch sides and lower rear, $\frac{1}{2}$ inch upper nose, $\frac{3}{8}$ inch deck, floor and turret top and $\frac{3}{4}$ inch upper rear. *Engine:* one Continental W670-9A radial, 250hp. *Length:* 14 feet 10 inches. *Height:* 7 feet 4 inches *Width:* 7 feet 6 inches

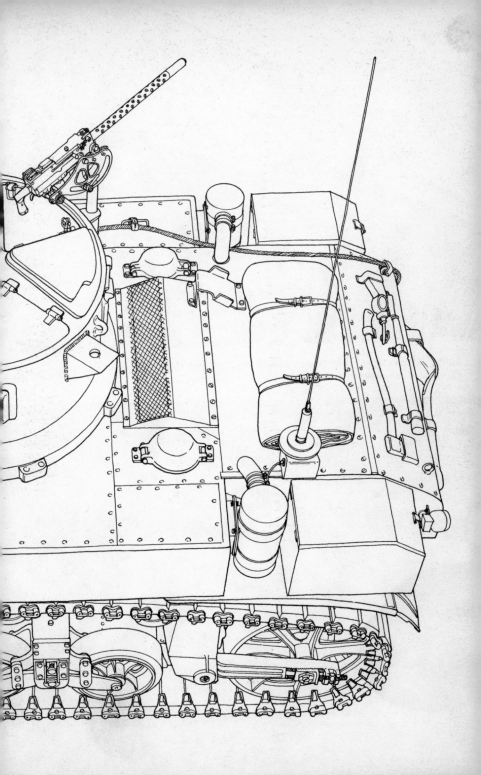

Above: Stuart light tanks helped to win the Battle of Tenaru for the Americans. Afterwards they were less effective. Below: Henderson Field

mined than ever to retake the island and to save face in the process by inflicting as decisive a victory as possible on the Americans. Operation *Ka* was far from over. The Marine Commander looked to land and sea forces for assistance. Marine Corps engineers struggled with captured Japanese equipment to make the airstrip serviceable and as early as 12th August a Catalina flying boat piloted by an aide to Rear-Admiral McCain who was in charge of land-based air operations, landed at the airfield. The aide then inspected the strip. It was only 2,600 feet long, it had no steel matting covering or taxiways and there was no drainage system. Depending upon the weather the airfield was usually either a swamp or a dust bowl. Nevertheless the aide pronounced it fit for fighter aircraft operations.

The airstrip, soon to be named Henderson Field after a hero of Midway, received its first contingent of operational aircraft on 20th August, in time for them to join in the mopping-up operations after the Battle of Tenaru. There were thirty-one aeroplanes, delivered as far as the waters off San Cristobal by the converted carrier *Long Island*. They were a welcome sight to the marines below as they made a circuit of the beachhead area before coming in to land. Twelve Marine Dauntless dive-bombers were commanded by Major Richard Mangrum, and nineteen Marine Wildcat fighters were under the supervision of Captain John Smith. There were not many of them but these aircraft were to have a spectacular effect upon the Guadalcanal campaign.

Vandegrift hoped that similar support would be coming from the Navy. It was certain that Japanese vessels would soon be landing reinforcements on Guadalcanal. These men in fact were already on their way. The remainder of Ichiki's force together with the 5th Special Naval Landing Force had been embarked at Truk on the transport *Kinryu Maru*

Admiral Tanaka

and four converted destroyers and were being conveyed to the Solomons by the veteran Rear-Admiral Raizo Tanaka. A much larger force would follow and, even more important, a large naval force was ordered to put to sea to destroy the American carriers reported somewhere between the Solomons and the New Hebrides, to bombard and destroy Henderson Field and to provide artillery fire to cover the men being conveyed by Admiral Tanaka. A dozen Japanese submarines were already lurking in the waters off Guadalcanal and Tulagi.

Intelligence reports informed Vandegrift that a large enemy naval force had assembled at Rabaul and was now heading for Guadalcanal. It was not at first appreciated just how large this armada was. There were two task forces consisting altogether of three aircraft carriers, eight battleships, four heavy cruisers, two light cruisers, twenty-one destroyers and a number of other vessels, sailing under an umbrella of air support provided

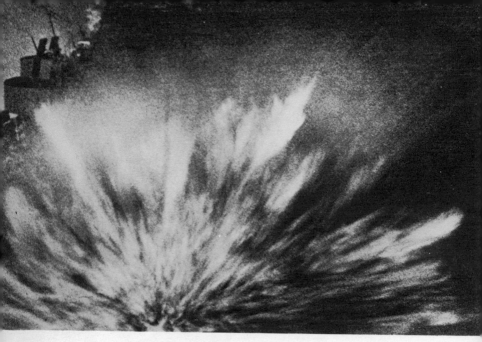

The Battle of the Eastern Solomons. *Above:* A bomb explodes on the carrier *Enterprise. Above right: Saratoga* moored with a 9½ degree list after the battle. *Below: Ryujo,* which was sunk by American aircraft

by aircraft of the 25th Air Flotilla based on Rabaul. The American naval forces were at this time cruising about one hundred miles south-east of Guadalcanal. Admiral Fletcher had in his command three aircraft carriers, one battleship, four cruisers and ten destroyers. American patrol planes spotted different Japanese vessels on 23rd and 24th August, while Japanese observer aircraft recognised the American force on 24th August.

The Battle of the Eastern Solomons which developed about two hundred miles from Guadalcanal was in one major respect like Midway. All the action took place between attacking aircraft and ships. No surface vessels came into contact with each other. Unlike Midway, the Battle of the Eastern Solomons was not a clear cut American victory, turning out to be something of a stalemate. On 24th August thirty-eight Dauntless and Avenger aircraft from the carrier *Saratoga* attacked and sank the Japanese carrier *Ryujo*. On the same afternoon Japanese aircraft attacked the American carrier *Enterprise*. Fletcher had taken the precaution of

maintaining fifty-three Wildcats in the air above the aircraft carrier. These planes swooped on the Japanese Zeros, Kates and Vals, while the carrier's anti-aircraft guns opened up at the same time. A terrific dog-fight took place over that area of the Pacific. The *Enterprise* was badly damaged but managed to limp away, escorted by various cruisers and destroyers, while the Japanese aircraft were forced to return to their own carriers.

There were other casualties in the Battle of the Eastern Solomons. In addition to the *Ryujo* the Japanese lost a destroyer and a cruiser, while the seaplane carrier *Chitose* and a cruiser were damaged. Ninety Japanese aircraft were shot down, to the American total of twenty. Admiral Fletcher withdrew his vessels later on the afternoon of 24th August, expecting to return and resume the battle the following day, but the Japanese also broke off the engagement and steamed out of range. The Battle of the Eastern Solomons had come to an inconclusive end.

Before the *Ryujo* had been attacked

Curtiss P-40. *Engine:* Allison V-1710, 1,040 hp at 15,000 feet. *Armament:* six .5-inch Browning machine guns. *Speed:* 357 mph at 15,000 feet. *Climb:* 3,080 feet per minute initially. *Ceiling:* 32,750 feet. *Range:* 1,400 miles maximum. *Weight empty/loaded:* 5,376/7,215 lbs. *Span:* 37 feet 4 inches. *Length:* 31 feet 9 inches

The Grumman F4F Wildcat was the best fighter aircraft available to the US Navy at the beginning of the Pacific campaign, and US pilots flying the type soon evolved tactics for dealing with the more manoeuvrable Zero *Engine* · Pratt & Whitney R-1830 radial, 1,200 hp. *Armament:* Six .5-inch machine guns and two 100 pound bombs. *Maximum speed:* 328 mph at 21,000 feet. *Climb:* 2,265 feet per minute. *Ceiling:* 37,500 feet. *Range:* 845 miles. *Weights empty/loaded:* 5,342/8,152 pounds. *Span:* 38 feet. *Length:* 28 feet 9 inches

The Douglas SBD Dauntless was used by the US Navy, Marines and Army (in service with the last it was designated A-24) and was remarkably successful wherever it was used. The bomb was carried on a crutch below the fuselage so that it would swing out past the propeller before being released and thus minimise any chance of damage to that vital component.

Specification for SBD-5. *Engine:* Wright R-1820 radial, 1,200 hp. *Armament:* Two .5-inch and two .3-inch machine guns plus a 1,000 pound bomb load. *Maximum speed:* 252 mph at 13,800 feet. *Climb:* 1,700 feet per minute. *Ceiling:* 24,300 feet. *Range:* 1,115 miles with 1,000 pound bomb. *Weights empty/loaded:* 6,533/10,700 pounds. *Span:* 41 feet 6 inches. *Length:* 33 feet

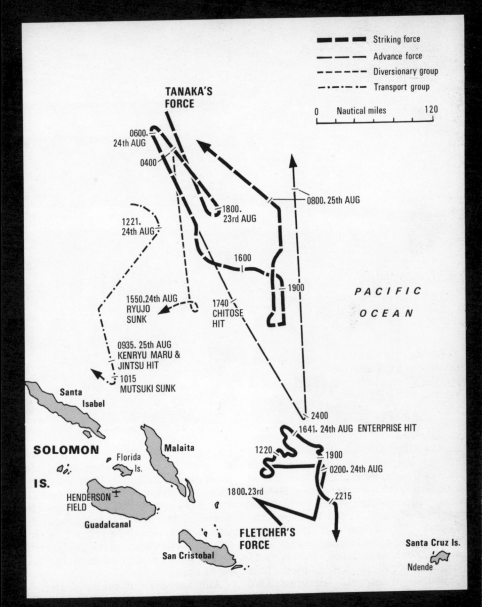

Striking force
Advance force
Diversionary group
Transport group

0   Nautical miles   120

TANAKA'S FORCE

0600. 24th AUG

0400

1800. 23rd AUG

0800. 25th AUG

1600

1900

1221. 24th AUG

1550. 24th AUG RYUJO SUNK

1740 CHITOSE HIT

0935. 25th AUG KENRYU MARU & JINTSU HIT

1015 MUTSUKI SUNK

PACIFIC OCEAN

Santa Isabel

2400

1641. 24th AUG ENTERPRISE HIT

SOLOMON

Malaita

1220

1900

0200. 24th AUG

Florida Is.

IS.

HENDERSON FIELD

1800. 23rd

2215

Guadalcanal

FLETCHER'S FORCE

Santa Cruz Is.

San Cristobal

Ndende

The Battle of the Eastern Solomons, 23rd August 1942

by American aircraft she had flown off twenty-one of her own planes to attack Guadalcanal. These were joined by a few Betty bombers from Rabaul and headed for Henderson Field. They were met by Wildcats from the Cactus Air Force on Henderson. Sixteen Japanese aircraft were shot down. Four days later aircraft from Henderson Field intercepted four Japanese transports carrying 3,500 troops. The destroyer *Asagiri* was blown up, *Yugiri* was set ablaze and *Shirakuma* damaged.

The conditions under which the pilots and ground crews worked in the early days at Henderson were abysmal. They were made no better by lack of foresight in Washington, notably by General Arnold's predilection for the P-40. This aircraft demanded high-pressure oxygen to be flown by its

pilots at high altitudes; there was no high pressure oxygen in bottled form on Guadalcanal. Restricted to a height of about ten thousand feet the P-40 was a sitting duck for any passing Zero. In the end Vandegrift ordered this aircraft to be equipped with a 500-pound bomb and to be used outside the perimeter area on bombing missions only.

Another case of faulty design for the conditions occurred in the SBD whose hard rubber tyres may have made it a suitable aircraft for landing on the deck of a carrier but which tore up the runway at Henderson. At the beginning there were no bomb hoists available and bombs had to be man-handled into position. Sweating ground staff also had to pump gasoline by hand from fifty-five gallon drums, taking several hours to refill a handful

This Japanese-built hut was used as Air Headquarters on Henderson Field

of planes. Added to this the living conditions of the pilots, forced to live in tents or, more often, in dug-outs and to eat rice, Spam and hash as a staple diet, were nothing to boast about.

Yet these men, living under these conditions did much to redress the balance of power on Guadalcanal. Certainly they did a great deal to prevent Vandegrift's marines being driven from their beachhead in the black days of August and September 1942. The pilots were brave and skilful and in the Grumman Wildcat they had an aeroplane worthy of them. In single combat a Wildcat might be no match for a Zero, but the Americans soon developed a system of two-plane flights, each aircraft looking after the other. If a single Wildcat did encounter a solitary Zero the accepted practice

was for the American aeroplane to empty its magazines in one quick burst and then make for Henderson as quickly as possible. Similarly any attacks on Japanese bombers were made from directly overhead or from high to one side, thus avoiding the enemy tail-gunner.

Slowly more aircraft began to arrive at Henderson Field. On 22nd August 5 Army P-40s landed. At 1430 on 30th August 31 aircraft flew in, under the overall command of Colonel Wallace. There were 19 F4F-4s led by Major Robert E Galer, and 12 SBD-3s led by Major L R Smith. By the end of August Guadalcanal possessed 64 American aircraft and 86 pilots.

The Tokyo Express

named 'Washing Machine Charlie' and 'Louie the Louse' droned ominously overhead. In addition there were well over 5,000 Japanese troops on Guadalcanal and the enemy seemed able to land more almost at will.

That the Japanese were able to reinforce their troops on Guadalcanal was due in a great measure to their supremacy at sea. Japanese vessels, although confining themselves mainly to night landings, were able to land companies of troops along the coast and then blast American shore installations on the return journey. Admiral Tanaka was to prove himself the most successful naval commander in the Pacific. Again and again he eluded American aircraft and surface vessels on his night runs until his convoys to Guadalcanal became so regular and so swift that they were known as 'The Tokyo Express'. Despite differences of opinion with General Kawaguchi and contradictory instructions from Rabaul, Tanaka successfully delivered Kawaguchi's force to Guadalcanal in the 'Rat' landing operations, and for the entire Guadalcanal campaign remained a thorn in the flesh of the Americans.

With Japanese forces being landed to both east and west of his perimeter area Vandegrift needed all the troops he could get. By the end of August the general was transferring troops from Tulagi to Guadalcanal, including Edson's Raiders. Vandegrift also began to make occasional cautious thrusts, especially in the area of Matanikau. After one inconclusive effort a second one was mounted on 27th August and entrusted to 1st Battalion, 5th Marines. While the 11th Marines maintained a heavy fire across the mouth of the Matanikau, most of the 1st Battalion embarked at the edge of the perimeter and travelled some distance along the coast, disembarking behind the Japanese front line. One company, in the

The aircraft flying their daily sorties from Henderson Field did a great deal to help the marines struggling to hold their perimeter on Guadalcanal, but at the beginning of September 1942, Vandegrift could not pretend that his position was a reassuring one. In the interest of speed he had embarked from New Zealand with sixty days' food supply instead of ninety, and half that food had not been unloaded. His hungry troops were stricken with dysentry and jungle-rot, although the worst effects of malaria would not make themselves felt until October. Few men could count on an undisturbed night's sleep as long as the Japanese prowler aircraft nick-

meantime, had advanced overland.

At 0730 the battalion landed and began to move east. 'C' Company was sent up to the ridge above the beach and ordered to move in a line parallel to the other companies advancing below. The terrain was rough and after an hour it became impossible for 'C' Company to keep up with the rest of the battalion. There was no radio communication and by 0930 contact between the troops on the ridge and those below had been lost. The battalion came to a halt and messengers were sent to fetch 'C' Company down to join the main body. In return the 1st Platoon 'B' Company and a machine gun platoon from

'D' Company were both sent up to the ridge. An hour later the battalion moved forward again only to run into fire from Japanese entrenched on the narrow strip of coastal plain. The marines returned the fire, using mortars, and dug themselves in after unsuccessfully attempting a flanking manoeuvre. The battalion commander decided that the intense heat and difficult terrain would make any further advance impossible and sent a radio message back to the perimeter requesting that boats be sent to a spot near Kokumbona to pick up his marines. An answer came almost at once from Colonel Hunt. The battalion commander was relieved of his

command which would pass to his second in command. There would be no evacuation. The attack would be pressed forward. Later in the day Hunt himself arrived and supervised the digging in for the night. The next morning the marines attacked only to find that the Japanese had withdrawn during the hours of darkness. The Americans then made their way to Matanikau village where boats picked them up and took them back to the perimeter area.

Vandegrift did not allow the failure of one mission to put him off. Early in September messages began to come through from Clemens and his scouts that about 300 well-armed Japanese

troops had gathered west of Tasimboko. Vandegrift entrusted to Edson and his men the task of destroying them. Edson, his Raiders recently brought over from Tulagi, planned the operation carefully. It would occupy only one day – 8th September. The destroyers transporting his force would give covering fire as the Americans disembarked east of Tasimoko and advanced westwards. Added protection would be provided by an airstrike from Henderson Field.

At 1800 on 7th September the Raiders went on board the destroyer-transports *Manley* and *McKean* and two small converted tuna fishing boats. At the last moment there had been a hitch when scouts had reported that there were now many more than the original 300 Japanese at Tasimboko, but Vandegrift and Edson decided to treat these reports as exaggerated. The 1st Parachute Battalion was moved to Lunga Point to sail in support the following day.

The landing area was reached at 0500 and small ships took the Raiders ashore. An accidental discharge of an American rifle caused some anxiety

The destroyer *McKean*, used to provide off-shore artillery

but there were no signs that the Japanese on the shore had heard anything. Once the Raiders were safely on the beach they fanned out in battle order to envelop the village. 'A' Company was on the left, 'B' Company remained on the beach, and 'C' Company moved forward into the jungle. At 0635 six aircraft left Henderson Field to carry out an air-strike west of the village. At the same time the two destroyer-trans-

USS *Fuller* – the Japanese thought she was bringing reinforcements

ports *Manley* and *McKean* began pumping shells into the area. At 0855 Edson reported light contact with the enemy but stated that the Japanese were withdrawing inland. He requested that air support be continued. This was granted. Two hours later Edson again made radio contact with the perimeter area, asking if more troops could be landed to reinforce him west of Tasimoko. Vandegrift answered that this was not possible and recommended that the Raiders withdraw and return to the *Manley* and *McKean*. It was confirmed, however, that the 1st Parachute Battalion was on its way, and this force in fact provided a flank and rear-

guard for the Raiders at Tasimboko.

At 1130 Edson reported that his men were under heavy artillery fire from the Japanese. He gathered his force together and advanced, only to discover that the enemy had withdrawn, leaving behind large quantities of food, ammunition and supplies, enough to suggest that 4,000 of Kawaguchi's soldiers had been there. The reason for the withdrawal of 4,000 Japanese in the face of less than 1,000 Americans was not established. It is possible that Kawaguchi wanted to concentrate on his main task of encircling and taking Henderson Field, and that he had no desire to be drawn into any other activities. Another reason advanced was that the chance appearance off the coast of the US ships *Fuller* and *Bellatrix* under destroyer escort persuaded the Japanese that a heavy landing was about to take place. In any event the Raiders' had a large cache of supplies to destroy or render useless before withdrawing to the beach and re-embarking for the perimeter area.

It was certainly true that Kawaguchi was making laborious but steady progress towards Henderson Field, his efforts sheltered from the eyes of American pilots by the thick jungle. In the Tasimboko area at this time were the headquarters of 35th Infantry Brigade, most of 124th Infantry, the second echelon of the Ichiki detachment and the survivors of the first Ichiki detachment. On the other side of the American perimeter, which was about two miles square, in the Kokumbona region (i.e. west of the perimeter) were the remainder of the 124th Infantry, the 11th and 13th Pioneers and members of a Special Naval Landing Force.

Since the beginning of September Kawaguchi's engineers had been cutting a road to Henderson Field from Tasimboko, using hand tools. As the road through the jungle progressed, infantry and artillery units followed the engineers. Reports from native scouts convinced Vandegrift that an

Brigadier-General Roy S Geiger

attack was coming from the east and he did his best with the resources available to strengthen his line of defence in the neighbourhood of Henderson Field. He was extremely limited in men and material. On 4th September two more ships, *Little* and *Gregory* had been shelled and sunk in Sealark Channel by vessels of Tanaka's Tokyo Express. The newly arrived commander of the 1st Air Wing, Brigadier-General Roy S Geiger, warned Vandegrift that the constant dog-fights had taken their toll of his

Lieutenant-Colonel Samuel B Griffith

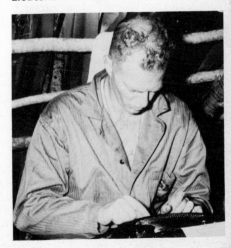

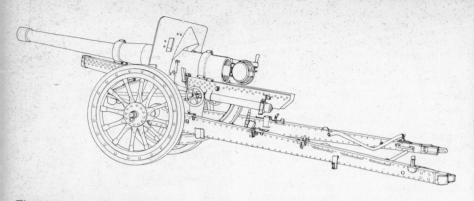

The Model 96 150mm howitzer was the standard Japanese medium howitzer, replacing the earlier Model 4 howitzer from 1937 onwards. It was moved as one load, pulled by a tractor. *Calibre:* 149.1mm. *Barrel length in calibres:* 23.37. *Maximum range:* 12,971 yards (pointed shell) and 11,336 yards (HE shell). *Elevation:* −5° to +65°. *Traverse:* 15° right and left. *Rate of fire:* 3 or 4 rounds per minute maximum. *Weight:* 9,108 lbs (firing) and 10,846 lbs (travelling). *Method of transport:* 5-ton tractor. *Time to emplace:* 7 minutes

aircraft. On 10th September only eleven of thirty-eight Wildcats were operational. For once one of Vandegrift's urgent requests was granted. Ghormley sent twenty-four more Wildcats to Henderson Field; they went into action almost immediately.

Also on 10th September Edson moved his mixed force of Raiders and Parachutists to a ridge about a mile south of Henderson Field, not far from Vandegrift's new headquarters. The Marine Commander had moved from a site north-west of the airstrip to be out of the direct path of Japanese air strikes. The ridge was about 1,000 yards long, running north-west to south-east, and was surrounded by steeply undulating dense jungle. It was here that the infiltrating Japanese were to come up against the marines in what was aptly to be named the Battle of Bloody Ridge.

The attack started on the morning of 11th September. Twenty-six Bettys bombed the ridge as marines were laying barbed wire and digging foxholes. Later that day Edson and his executive officer, Lieutenant-Colonel Samuel B Griffith, went half a mile to the south in order to look for any

signs of Japanese activity. They saw none, but Clemens and his scouts reported that a large force of the enemy was moving through the jungle. Edson saw to it that the Parachutists on the east flank and the Raiders in the centre and to the west of the ridge were at top alert, and settled down to wait.

Vandegrift had other problems. An ambiguous message had been received by Ghormley from Nimitz. Nimitz had requested that MacArthur receive from Ghormley a reinforced regiment of experienced amphibious troops. The only troops of this nature were struggling to maintain the precarious perimeter on Guadalcanal. Ghormley passed on the message to Admiral Turner, who was horrified. Far from removing a regiment from Vandegrift he should be given an additional one. Ghormley listened to Turner and then provided him with additional information. The Japanese attack on Guadalcanal was obviously going to be a major one. Ghormley did not think he had the material or the ships to be able to help the marines on the island.

This was the information with which

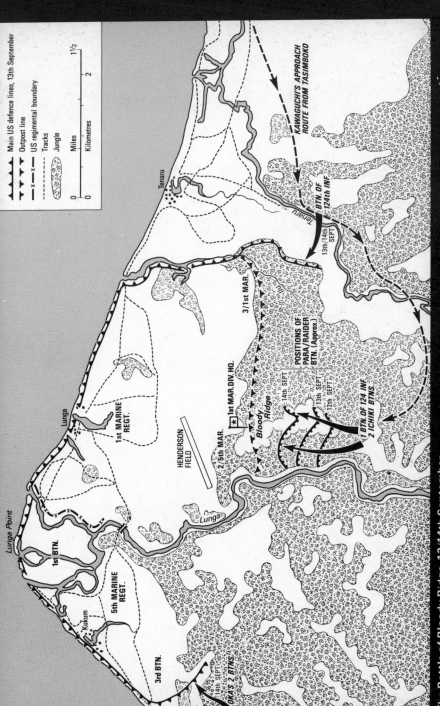

The Battle of Bloody Ridge, 12/14th September

Legend:
- Main US defence lines, 13th September
- Outpost line
- US regimental boundary
- Tracks
- Jungle

Miles: 0 — 1½
Kilometres: 0 — 2

Map labels:

Lunga Point

1st BTN.

5th MARINE REGT.

3rd BTN.

Kukum

OKA'S 2 BTNS.
14th SEPT

To Matanikau

Lunga

1st MARINE REGT.

HENDERSON FIELD

2/5th MAR.

★ 1st MAR. DIV. HQ.

Bloody Ridge

14th SEPT

13th SEPT

12th SEPT

POSITIONS OF PARA/RAIDER BTN. (Approx.)

1 BTN. OF 124 INF
2 ICHIKI BTNS.

3/1st MAR.

Tenaru

13th/14th SEPT

BTN. OF 124th INF

KAWAGUCHI'S APPROACH ROUTE FROM TASIMBOKO

Henderson Field after an air raid. The fuel drums in the foreground and the aircraft are being rolled to safety

Turner flew in to Guadalcanal on the morning of 11th September. It seemed as if Ghormley had written off any chance of the Guadalcanal campaign being successful. The few square miles of beachhead occupied by Vandegrift's marines and held at such great cost were about to be relinquished. Turner, however, was not so pessimistic. He promised Vandegrift that he would do everything in his power to ensure that the 7th Marines, formerly garrisoning Samoa, be sent to Guadalcanal. Vandegrift in turn determined that his men would hold the perimeter area as long as possible, but he instructed Geiger that in the event of the marines being pushed back the air force commander would fly his aircraft out of Guadalcanal. In the meantime Vandegrift would have to wait for Kawaguchi to make his move.

The Marine Commander did not know it but that move had been scheduled for 12th September. This was the date that Kawaguchi had set for his attack on Henderson Field. It was to be supported by naval gunfire and successive air attacks and would come from three directions. Kawaguchi himself would advance from south of the airfield with one battalion of the 124th Infantry and the two Ichiki battalions. Another battalion from the 124th Infantry would move west across the Tenaru while Colonel Oka led two battalions across the Lunga River and attacked the airstrip from the north-west. The plan was ambitious and a little too elaborate considering the conditions and terrain, but Kawaguchi had made up his mind to adhere to it. The jungle might slow his men up and the humidity cause them to drop beneath the weight of their equipment but the

Bloody Ridge after the battle. Here the Marines held off a Japanese attack and inflicted casualties of over 700

Blood Ridge – 'a sea of dead and wounded'

date of the attack would not be altered.

Edson deployed his 700 Raiders and Parachutists and a few Engineer and Pioneer personnel as best he could along the ridge he had selected as a likely spot for the Japanese to cross in their advance. Areas of the jungle were cleared and barbed wire strung from tree to tree to provide some sort of defence. Edson's command post was only a hundred yards from the one occupied by Vandegrift. In support were 105mm howitzers and the 2nd Battalion, 5th Marines. At 2100 the Japanese float plane nicknamed 'Louie the louse' dropped flares. At the same time a naval bombardment opened up from the sea. It lasted for twenty minutes. There was a pause and then the shelling started again. A Japanese cruiser and three destroyers were cruising up and down the shoreline in the vicinity of Tenaru, pumping shells into the American positions. The shelling stopped and then Japanese automatic and mortar fire from the troops on land began. There were the usual cries of 'Banzai!' and Japanese troops of the 124th Infantry poured out of the jungle, engulfing the Raiders and Parachutists guarding the perimeter of the ridge. The Americans fought back, wavered and then retreated. If Kawaguchi had only been able to maintain closer contact with his troops in the darkness in order to control their advance, the Americans might have been driven from the ridge and the control posts of both Vandegrift and Edson overrun. The situation became too chaotic for this. At one point Kawaguchi and a handful of aides became completely cut off from the remainder of his force. The confusion engendered by this enabled Edson to withdraw his troops in a more or less orderly fashion and take up a fresh defensive position on the ridge. He lost one platoon temporarily, adrift on the flank, but even these men managed to fight their way back to the high ground eventually.

At dawn Edson ordered a counterattack. The Japanese activity during the night and early morning had been intense but the colonel knew that it had not been a major thrust; after the initial impetus had failed it had become just another night attack. With the coming of daylight the enemy would probably withdraw to the shelter of the jungle, lick their wounds and wait for night to fall again. In order to encourage the Japanese to leave, the marines charged, cleared the ridge and retook their former position.

The day of 13th September, a Sunday, was spent by the weary Americans in consolidating their position. New foxholes were prepared, more wire laid. The Japanese sent in waves of strafing aircraft to make this work as difficult as possible, but the marines worked on, short of food and sleep but realising that the enemy would come again that night and that they had to be ready.

The Japanese attacked as expected. Again the noise was indescribable as seven of their destroyers opened up from the sea, raining shells on Henderson Field and its surrounds. 'Louie the Louse' made night day with its flares. Kawaguchi's charge, when it came, was straightforward, unsubtle and courageous. Advancing through smoke laid down, 2,000 men sprinted out of the jungle and up the slope leading to the ridge. The Americans poured small-arm and mortar fire into the advancing Japanese, hardly bothering to aim into the dense mass. Hundreds of men fell on the slopes but their comrades merely hurdled the fallen dead and wounded and kept on. Again the American line wavered. This time a handful of officers and NCOs were responsible for maintaining stability among the Raiders and Parachutists. Edson, 'Red Mike', was himself among the forward troops, encouraging and urging his men.

Major Kenneth Bailey, at first bringing up fresh supplies of grenades and ammunition, cut off many retreating marines, turning them back to face the Japanese and screaming the traditional Corps cry 'Do you want to live for ever'? Edson called for more artillery support. It was forthcoming and it was accurate. The colonel passed back the word. The range was perfect; it was knocking hell out of the Japanese.

The artillery fire drove the Japanese back. They regrouped and at 0200 they came again. At the same time, approximately, the Ishitari Battalion crossed the Tenaru (Ilu) and launched an attack against the positions held by 3rd Battalion, 1st Marines. The wire laid by the marines held the Japanese up and artillery fire decimated them.

On Bloody Ridge Edson shortened his line and called for still more artillery. The second Japanese attack was not as wholehearted as the first had been. Edson could sense victory. At 0230 he sent a message to Vandegrift assuring the general that the Americans on the ridge could hold their position. Vandegrift, as self-possessed as ever, coolly told a war correspondent 'It's only a few more hours to dawn. Then we'll see how we stand.' Still the Japanese came, in waves and as single snipers. Three of them broke into Vandegrift's command post but were shot down by guards and Marine clerks. The Japanese began to fall back again, broken. Colonel Watanabe had not pressed his attack on Henderson Field. Colonel Oka's attack, when it came, was to be too little and too late. Kawaguchi knew that he was defeated. By the morning of 14th September the survivors of his force were retreating through the jungle towards the Matanikau.

The marines came out blinking into the morning sunlight. Bloody Ridge was a sea of dead and wounded. Fifty-nine Americans had died and 204 had been wounded. The Japanese killed amounted to over 700. Briefly Vande-

grift considered pursuing the enemy but decided against it. Many of his marines had not slept for three days and nights. Henderson Field had been secured against attack; the general was content. There were snipers to be mopped up and the wounded to be treated with caution, but the Battle of Bloody Ridge was over and it had been a significant victory for the Americans.

It was followed almost at once by a defeat, as usual at sea. On the morning of 14th September, as the marines were consolidating their position around Henderson Field, Admiral Turner was keeping his promise and bringing the 7th Marines to Guadalcanal from the New Hebrides where they had been sent after their stint on Samoa. Turner had prevailed over the cautious Ghormley and obtained the use of this fresh and untried force. The escort force consisted of Turner in his flagship *McCawley*, a carrier force including *Wasp* and *Hornet* commanded by Rear-Admiral Leigh Noyes, and other vessels. Towards the end of the morning the force was seen by a

Japanese aircraft. Turner maintained course until nightfall but then withdrew in *McCawley*, taking with him the six precious transports, containing 4,000 marines. The carriers *Wasp* and *Hornet* held their course, escorted by the battleship *North Carolina* and various cruisers and destroyers. On 15th September, just before 0230 two Japanese submarines, the I-19 and the I-15, attacked the group. The I-19 struck the *Wasp* with three torpedoes. The I-15 missed its target, the *Hornet*, but struck *North Carolina* instead, opening up a hole thirty feet by eighteen feet in its side below the waterline. In the resultant confusion the destroyer *O'Brien* was also torpedoed and later sank. *Wasp* was crippled and out of control. A series of explosions tore the carrier from stem to stern. 193 men of the ship's company of over 2,000 had been killed. Captain Sherman held a hasty consultation with his officers on the flight deck and gave the order to abandon ship. Life-rafts were lowered and many men jumped over the side of *Wasp* into the water to be picked up by escort vessels. Acting upon the orders of Rear-Admiral Scott, now in charge of the force, the destroyer *Lansdowne* approached the helplessly drifting *Wasp* and fired five torpedoes into her and sank her. The action off the Santa Cruz islands was over.

Left top and middle: The destroyer *O'Brien* hit by a torpedo on 15th September 1942. *USS Wasp* burns in the background. *Left bottom:* The end of the *Wasp. Below:* USS North Carolina

Above: Badly-needed reinforcements arrive on Guadalcanal in September.
Below: Fresh supplies are unloaded at Lunga Point

American Naval forces had suffered another blow at the hands of the Japanese.

Fortunately for Vandegrift, despite the loss of *Wasp*, *O'Brien* and, for a time, *North Carolina*, the transports containing the 4,000 men of the 7th Marines reached Guadalcanal safely, vindicating the decision to detach *McCawley* and the transports from the carrier force. The newcomers came ashore in their clean utility suits and new helmets to join the dirty, exhausted and malaria-ridden Marines already on Guadalcanal, veterans after only six weeks. As Admiral Turner disembarked the reinforcements, he ordered the destroyers *Monssen* and *MacDonough* to shell Japanese positions along the coast as some slight return for the almost nightly shellings of the Tokyo Express.

It was at this time that the coastwatchers Rhoades and Schroeder were rescued from their increasingly dangerous position on the north-west coast of Guadalcanal. There were now far too many Japanese in position in this region and it looked increasingly probable that some of them would stumble across the coastwatchers, despite the loyalty of the islanders. In order to effect their rescue another coastwatcher, D C Horton who had gone ashore with the marines at Tulagi, borrowed a launch and negotiated Japanese held waters by night until he reached a creek in the area of the north-west coast. Here he took on board not only Rhoades and Schroeder but also thirteen missionaries, a shot down American airman and Rhoades' radio-telephone, making the return trip to Lunga in safety.

Vandegrift continued to send out patrols. In the dense jungles they were his only eyes and ears for the aircraft could not penetrate the trees and undergrowth. Vandegrift had to know what the Japanese were doing. He had some 19,000 men confined in the beachhead area some three miles long and extending little over a mile into

Lieutenant-Colonel 'Chesty' Puller

the bush, as the natives called the jungle. The Battle of Bloody Ridge had taken off the pressure to a certain extent, but the air strikes from Rabaul were coming as regularly as ever and his patrols were still being ambushed whenever they left the perimeter area. On 25th September Rabaul had received reinforcements amounting to 100 Zeros and 80 bombers; these were thrown at Guadalcanal almost at once. In one raid alone 23 out of 60 Japanese aircraft were knocked out of the sky by the aircraft based at Henderson Field. At the end of September three of the Marine pilots from this airstrip were the leading aces in the US armed forces: Major John Smith had destroyed 19 Japanese aircraft, Captain Marion Carl had 16 'kills' to his credit, while Captain Robert Galer had shot down 11 Japanese attackers. It was Carl who had been shot down and who had made his way back through the enemy lines only to be told that while he had been trudging through the bush Smith had gone ahead in the table of Japanese aeroplanes destroyed. 'Dammit!' Carl had protested, 'Ground him for five days!'

Vandegrift relied on the fliers but

did his best to ensure that his ground troops would also continue to give a good account of themselves. Throughout the latter half of September he consolidated the gains made immediately after the Battle of Bloody Ridge, advancing to the south a few hundred yards and seeing to it that he now had a constant line of defence around the airfield instead of a series of strong points linked by patrols as before. Trees were felled and grass burned to give his gunners a wider field of fire. Mines were laid and booby traps prepared at all approaches to the perimeter. The area was strong, Vandegrift was convinced of that.

But he was still fighting a defensive war, clinging to a pitifully small perimeter. One day he would have to advance. Before he could do that he would have to cross the Matanikau for good, not merely drive the Japanese back, because the Japanese always returned to this muddy and sluggish river, hidden by the trees growing up to the banks.

Above: A US 155mm howitzer shells Jap positions, mid — September 1942. *Right:* A wounded Marine is carried back from the frontline

It was along the Matanikau that the 1st Battalion, 7th Marines made its first major contact with the enemy. On the afternoon of 21st September the battalion made its way, under Lieutenant-Colonel Lewis 'Chesty' Puller, towards the head of the river. Japanese rifle and mortar fire took its toll of the inexperienced marines. For two days Puller tried to take his men across the Matanikau, moving up and down the banks of the river trying to find a place to ford. For two days the Japanese picked off his marines until Puller was forced to pull his men back and report to Vandegrift that the Japanese were assembled in force on the far side of the Matanikau. This news indicated to the general that the lull after Bloody Ridge was over. The general had even started to live in

comparative comfort; his control post had been wired for electricity. Vandegrift decided that an operation should be mounted to drive the Japanese back from the Matanikau. He ordered the 1st Raiders, now commanded by Colonel Samuel Griffiths, to penetrate inland along the east bank of the river and to cross by a log bridge upstream. They would then turn and return the way they had come on the west bank, attacking the Japanese and driving them into the sea. Their attack would be the signal for 2nd Battalion, 5th Marines to charge across the sandbank at the mouth of the river. While this was happening Puller's 1st Battalion, 7th Marines would be landed behind the Japanese at Point Cruz and attack from the rear along a coastal track.

The Japanese were waiting for the Americans when they made their move on 27th September. Griffith's battalion was pinned down by heavy fire and could not cross the log bridge. Griffith was wounded and Major Bailey, the hero of Bloody Ridge and before that of the Tulagi landing was killed. Only three days before Bailey had said to a war correspondent of his troops 'You get to know these kids so well when you're working with 'em, and they're such swell kids that when it comes to a job that's pretty rugged, you'd rather go yourself than send them.'

Edson, who was in charge of the whole operation, was given to understand that Griffith's men had in fact successfully crossed the Matanikau. He gave the order for 2nd Battalion, 5th Marines to charge across the sand-

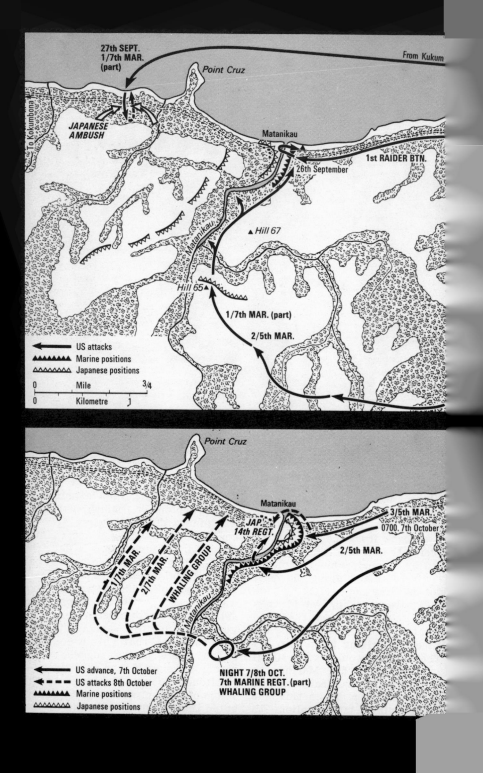

bank. Again the Japanese were ready and there was no distracting attack, from up river. The Japanese drove the Americans back across the sandbank. To make matters even worse, Puller's Marines had landed at Point Cruz, advanced 400 yards and walked into a Japanese ambush. Puller was not with his men as he had been detached to aid Edson, but the acting commander, Major Otho Rogers, was killed. The Japanese closed in, killing many Americans. Everything was going wrong. A heavy Japanese air raid destroyed communications and a message from Edson calling for air support for the men trapped at Point Cruz did not get through. Puller left Edson and boarded the destroyer *Ballard* and ordered it to steam at top speed to Point Cruz. As soon as *Ballard* got within range it began shelling the Japanese while signalmen on the destroyer ordered the ambushed marines to fight their way back to the beach. At the same time American artillery also began to get the range of the Japanese.

Frantically the Marines clawed their way back to the beach. Again there were individual acts of heroism. A coast-guard coxswain, Donald Munro, guided the first of the landing boats ashore from the destroyer, steering with one hand and firing at the enemy with the other. He was killed as was Platoon Sergeant Anthony P Malinowski Jnr of 'A' Company who covered the retreat of his comrades with a Browning automatic rifle. Another act of bravery was that of Sergeant Robert D Raysbrook who continued to receive and transmit semaphore messages to the destroyer under heavy fire.

The marines took up a defensive position on the beach and hoped that the landing boats would reach them. For a time it was a near thing. Japanese artillery fire from Point Cruz to the east and Kukumbona to the west drove the boats back. For a time the coxswains wavered. Then an SBD pilot, Lieutenant Dale M Leslie, the man who had first seen the trapped marines and radioed the news to Edson, swooped low over the landing craft time and time again, guiding them in to the beach. He then left the beach area and began strafing enemy positions a little way inland. Eventually the marines at Point Cruz were ferried out to *Ballard*. They had lost twenty-four men killed and twenty-three wounded. The Americans broke off the action all the way along the Matanikau, giving up their plan to cross to the east bank. They had suffered a defeat and lost sixty dead and a hundred wounded in the process.

Vandegrift persevered with his intention of clearing the far bank of the Matanikau. He had a great deal on his mind at the end of September and the beginning of October. Turner was writing letters suggesting future operations, to the general's considerable annoyance. Vandegrift wrote back shortly, rejecting the admiral's suggestions. In the same week the general had another encounter with the top brass. Nimitz, Commander-in-Chief, Pacific Ocean Area, landed at Henderson Field in a Flying Fortress for consultations with Vandegrift and Geiger. The two men did their best to brief the Commander-in-Chief on his flying visit and had a bad moment when the admiral's aircraft almost crashed upon take-off.

Important as these confrontations and consultations were they were mere side issues when compared with the immediate task of holding the beachhead. The rainy season was fast approaching and Vandegrift could guess what it would be like fighting in the steaming jungles when the monsoons hit the island. At the beginning of October he ordered another expedition to clear the Japanese from the west bank of the Matanikau River. His tactics were not very different from previous attempts. First of all patrol activity would take place in order to try and estimate the number of Japanese to be faced. Intelligence for the previous attack had been poor. After it was all over Colonel Griffith was to write 'No orders would ever have been given for a battalion to go up to Kokumbona had there been any realization that there were several thousand Japanese between the Matanikau and Kokumbona.' This time Vandegrift wanted there to be no mistakes.

The operation was scheduled to begin on 7th October when the forces concerned would take up their positions. The 5th Marines (without 1st Battalion) would spread out along the west bank of the river. Colonel William J Whaling would then take the 3rd Battalion, 2nd Marines across the Matanikau together with a detachment of his own Scout-Snipers, turn north and march towards the sea. The 1st and 2nd Battalions of the 7th Marines would follow, each in turn penetrating a little further west before turning. When Colonel Puller's 1st Battalion reached and took Point Cruz it would be the signal for Edson's men to cross the Matanikau while Whaling and Puller enveloped the Japanese. The whole operation would be supported by aircraft from the 1st Marine Air Wing which would dive bomb and machine gun Japanese positions.

The operation began at 0700 on 7th October. At 1000 the 3rd Battalion of the 5th Marines, advancing towards the east bank of the Matanikau, ran into sporadic Japanese fire which continued for most of the day without seriously impeding the Americans. They reached the banks of the river as intended and dug in. The 2nd Battalion, 5th Marines took up its position to the left of the 3rd Battalion without encountering opposition. The 7th Marines and the Scout-Snipers also reached the east bank preparatory to crossing. The only serious opposition was encountered towards the end of the day by the 3rd Battalion, 5th Marines which surrounded a detachment of Japanese troops who refused to surrender.

The 8th October was a day of pouring rain. The troops whose job it was to wait on the east bank of the Matanikau did so in conditions of great discomfort and misery. Whaling's group pressed across the river on its march past Matanikau village. At dusk on the 8th the Japanese who had been surrounded on the east bank of the river attempted to break out. At first their attempt looked like being successful. They killed a dozen Raiders and made for the sandbank at the mouth of the Matanikau. Here, however, they became entangled in the wire barricade strung by the Americans. As the Japanese struggled to penetrate the wire the Americans poured a withering fire into them. Sixty-seven of the Japanese were killed before dawn.

Whaling and Puller continued on their march only to receive an urgent message from Vandegrift. There had been a sudden change of plan. A coastwatcher had reported from Rabaul that a Japanese invasion fleet was massing, apparently to proceed to Guadalcanal. The American commander dared not string his forces out too far. He ordered Whaling and Puller to continue with their encircling movement but that as soon as they had made their turn they were to return to the perimeter. Even if they defeated the Japanese they were not to pursue them to the west. Vandegrift added that the 5th Marines would not now be crossing the Matanikau but would remain on the east bank to give the returning marines covering fire when they had fought their way back.

In spite of the abrupt change of plans the move was successful. On 9th October both Whaling and Puller turned and headed back towards the Matanikau's west bank. Whaling's men attacked along the coastal track and forced their way through to the river. Puller and the 1st Battalion, 7th Marines were even more spectacularly successful. Smarting from their reverse at Point Cruz ten days before, they obtained their revenge in

no uncertain manner. Puller had been leading his men back towards the Matanikau in accordance with his instructions, keeping to the high ground, when a section of the Japanese 4th Infantry Regiment had attacked. Puller's men had been in a commanding position on the top of a ridge while the Japanese had been forced to scramble up a steep ravine in order to get at the Americans. The marines kept their heads and cut the Japanese down as they staggered up the incline. The Japanese had broken and fled but then regrouped and attacked again, only to meet another fusilade of fire from the well-protected marines. For a second time the Japanese, or those that survived, fled down the ravine. This time they were trapped in the

An improvised radio station in operation

valley below. Desperately they tried to escape by climbing up the slope on the opposite side. Puller merely directed his fire across the intervening space. Over 600 Japanese were killed and the 1st Battalion, 7th Marines reached the Matanikau and crossed back to the American perimeter.

It later transpired that the large number of Japanese troops on the west bank of the Matanikau had been due to the fact that the Japanese had themselves been about to attack across the river. The American advance had broken up this attack before it could be started.

Dugout Sunday

predictions, but every man out there, ashore or afloat, will give a good account of himself.'

There was a public clamour for information. Newspapers ran editorials reflecting the uncertainty of the situation. The censored reports of the handful of war correspondents in the Solomons were avidly read. The days were gone when Admiral King could testily reply to a request for information: 'Tell 'em when it's over; then tell 'em who won.' In the sudden spotlight certain facts were revealed, both to the public and to political leaders. The makeshift character of the whole Guadalcanal operation to date could not be entirely hidden, nor could the lack of confidence in the campaign of some of its planners be denied. Changes were demanded and they were forthcoming. President Roosevelt himself requested the Joint Chiefs of Staff to send all available aid to Guadalcanal. It was announced that Ghormley was to be replaced as Commander of the South Pacific Area by the more aggressive Vice-Admiral William F Halsey. 'Bull' Halsey was noted for his vitriolic speech and conviction that attack was the best form of defence; it was hoped that he would bring a little more fire to the council tables of the Guadalcanal operation.

It was also decided to send army units to reinforce Vandegrift's marines. So far the only other ground unit in the Solomons in any size were the 'Seabees', the Sixth Naval Construction Battalion. For some time the marines had been putting disparaging words to the tune of 'Bless 'Em All'

Oh, we asked for the army to come to
                                    Tulagi
But Douglas MacArthur said, 'No!'
He gave as his reason,
'This isn't the season'.
'Besides, there is no USO.'
Now this was to be remedied. One of

It was half way through October and the marines had been on Guadalcanal for some nine weeks. Slowly, through a cloud of official reticence, the American public began to realise that their troops were fighting for their lives on some obscure island in the south-west Pacific, and that a major campaign, not a hit-and-run raid, was under way. It was also becoming apparent that the marines were in a tough spot. At a mid-October news conference in Washington, Navy Secretary Knox was asked if the Americans could hold Guadalcanal. His answer was honest if hardly reassuring: 'I certainly hope so. I expect so. I don't want to make any

Admiral Halsey takes the oath

Ghormley's last actions before handing over to Halsey had been to accede to the request of Major-General Millard Harmon to be allowed to strengthen the garrison on Guadalcanal. On 8th October, the 164th Infantry Regiment of the Americal Division embarked at Noumea to be transported by Admiral Turner to Guadalcanal.

The Japanese were now taking Guadalcanal as seriously as the Americans. Both Colonel Ichiki and General Kawaguchi had failed to drive the Americans from the perimeter or even to take Henderson Field. The Japanese High Command blamed the 'bamboo spear' or primitive fighting methods of both commanders. Such tactics would not again be employed. Lieutenant-General Hyakutake put off his plans to attack Port Moresby and decided that Guadalcanal would be the number one priority. He would lead the attacking force himself, reinforcing the troops already on the island with the famous Sendai Division and other units.

In order to make sure that his men reached Guadalcanal safely Hyakutake demanded that the naval forces escorting his division be of the highest standard. His request and the implication that previous escorts had not been good enough, offended the naval authorities but they agreed to provide him with four battleships and a number of lighter vessels and to send six more submarines to the Solomons area. In addition, Captain Ohmae, in charge of naval planning at Rabaul, pointed out that in order to give the general's troops a free run on Guadalcanal, Henderson Field would have to be destroyed. A certain amount of destruction could be wrought from the sea and air but in order to complete the task a heavy land bombardment would also be needed. Ohmae offered to provide General Hyakutake with a seaplane tender and an escort of two destroyers to take a number of heavy artillery guns, including the

one later to be nicknamed 'Pistol Pete' by the Americans, to Guadalcanal. Hyakutake accepted the offer appreciatively.

On 7th October, Rear-Admiral Norman Scott took a small naval force from the New Hebrides to a position near the Russell Islands in the Solomons. His vessels were the advance guard of the convoy which was to bring the men of the Americal Division to Guadalcanal. Scott had also been ordered to do his best to harry any Japanese shipping bringing men and supplies from Rabaul and the Western Solomons to Guadalacanal. His force consisted of the heavy cruisers *San Francisco* and *Salt Lake City;* the light cruisers *Helena* and *Boise;* and the destroyers *Buchanan, Duncan, Farenholt, Laffey* and *McCalla.*

At 1345 on 11th October, Scott received a message to the effect that a force of enemy cruisers and destroyers was moving down the Slot, heading for Guadalcanal. It was, in fact part of the Tokyo Express under Admiral Goto moving down to shell Henderson Field. Hyakutake had been landed on Guadalcanal several days previously with his senior staff officers, just in time for the general to hear of Puller's success against the 4th Infantry. Now the Japanese navy was keeping its promise to give the army plenty of support.

At 1810 Scott received another message. The Japanese ships were now only 110 miles away. Scott set out to meet them, estimating that he should intercept the Japanese off Cape Esperance at about midnight.

At 2230 he sent his float planes off into the night on a search-and-locate mission. An aeroplane from *Salt Lake City* caught alight from its own flares and was hastily pushed over the side, continuing to burn in the water. The blazing wreckage was seen from a distance by Admiral Goto on his flagship *Aoba* and was mistaken for a signal light from the shore. A few minutes later both *Helena* and *Boise* made radar contact with the enemy.

The heavy cruiser, *USS San Francisco,*
which took part in the battle

The Battle of Cape Esperance was
about to begin. It was characterised
on both sides by confusion and hesi-
tancy. Admiral Scott, possessing the
initial advantages of surprise and
position, almost threw them away.
His vessels had unwittingly crossed
the 'T' of the Japanese formation,
catching the enemy broadside on, a
classic naval manouevre. Unfortunately Scott was not sure which were
his vessels and which the enemy's.
The official report of the Strategic
Bombing Survey was to say, 'the
United States commander was unable
to visualize the situation since the
flagship was not equipped with the
most recent radar.' There was also a
mix-up in the signals between Captain
Hoover of *Helena* and Scott which
resulted in *Helena* holding her fire
until it was almost too late. Shortly
before 2300, however, the signal was
given and the six inch guns of the

Helena blasted at *Aoba,* severely
damaging the flagship and mortally
injuring Admiral Goto.

Too late, the Japanese fought back.
The destroyer *Fubuki* was sunk
and the cruiser *Furutaka* so badly
shelled that she sank several hours
later. The Japanese vessels scattered
and brought their own guns to bear,
sinking *Duncan* and badly damaging
Boise and *Farenholt.* The action was
not long drawn-out, neither was it as
decisive as the Battle of Savo, but it
resulted in a slight advantage for the
Americans, especially as the Japanese
destroyers *Murakakumo* and *Natsu-
gumo,* breaking off from the action,
were sunk the following day by American aircraft.

The American victory, such as it
was, was largely a technical one. It
may have delayed the Tokyo Express,
it did not stop it. Scott's vessels were
in no condition to continue to fight off
any advancing naval force. The Japanese were able to continue with their
scheme. On 13th October Japanese

Above: Japanese transports on fire after attacks by American aircraft, 16th October
Below: Japanese shipping in Bougainville attacked, 13th October

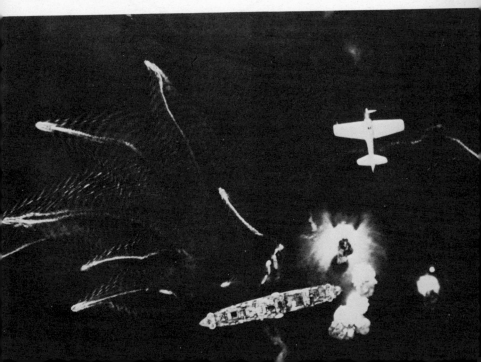

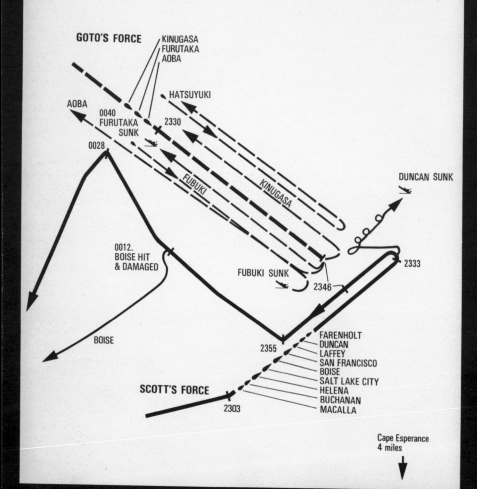

The Battle of Cape Esperance, 11/12th October 1942

heavy artillery opened up on Henderson Field, quickly finding the range and making it impossible for aircraft to take off. An alternate airstrip had been prepared south of Henderson Field and fighters were able to use this. The land barrage was only a preliminary. Later that night a powerful Japanese naval force approached Guadalcanal unopposed and began to pump shells into the airfield and its perimeter. The battleships *Kongo* and *Haruna*, the light cruiser *Isuzu* and eight destroyer escorts cruised up and down the coast of the island. In eighty minutes 918 rounds of 15 inch, 6 inch and 5 inch ammunition were fired by the battleships, tearing up the airfield and killing forty Americans.

The following morning only forty-two aircraft could fly and Henderson Field was out of action, a place of smouldering wooden buildings and gaping holes. The denizens of the area emerged from their foxholes and set about repairing the damage.

When dawn broke on 15th October it could be seen that the Japanese navy had taken advantage of the crippled state of the American air service on Guadalcanal. Five Japanese transports, escorted by eleven destroyers and other vessels were unloading at Tassafaronga, ten miles from Lunga Point. This time the Japanese had been over-optimistic. The American fliers had been only temporarily grounded. Ground crews searched frantically for fuel, draining the tanks of crashed aircraft, unearthing hidden caches until 400 drums, enough for two days, had been accumulated and man-handled to the waiting aircraft. At the same time, in response to urgent requests from Vandegrift and Geiger, C-47s began flying in fuel from the New Hebrides and transport vessels also began to carry the precious life-blood of the aircraft. One transport, *MacFarland*, was bombed in Sealark Channel but its crew managed to run the vessel ashore.

Staggering off the ground as best they could the American aeroplanes left Henderson Field and the adjacent fighter strip and headed for the transports at Tassafaronga. They sank one, damaged two and drove the rest out to sea where they sank another. It was a gesture but little more because the Japanese had landed the 4,000 men the transports had been carrying and the greater part of the consignment of food, weapons and ammunition. The latest Japanese arrivals, men of the 230th Infantry of the 38th Division and seven companies of the 16th Infantry of the 2nd Division, brought the total Japanese armed forces on Guadalcanal to something in excess of 20,000, roughly the same amount as the Americans had.

The Japanese, however, were fresher and better equipped. Vandegrift witnessed the arrival of the enemy reinforcements and knew that a major offensive was on the way. He put in yet another request for assistance, categorising his present strength as 'totally inadequate'. The Chiefs of Staff, immersed in other theatres of operations as well as the Pacific, could do little more than send a few more aircraft to the New Hebrides where they came under the command of Rear-Admiral Aubrey W Fitch who had taken over as commander of the land-based aircraft in the South Pacific, and to patch up the carrier *Enterprise* and send her with *South Dakota* and nine destroyers from Pearl Harbor to Guadalcanal.

Hyakutake had some cause to be satisfied. Both his men and his heavy artillery were safely on the island. He could proceed with his plan to take Henderson Field. The brunt of the attack would fall to the lot of the Sendai Division. This force, under Lieutenant-General Masao Maruyama, would move inland from Kokumbona until it was in position south of Henderson Field. It would then split up into two sections, the right wing consisting of the 29th Infantry under General Kawaguchi, and the left under

Major-General Yumio Nasu. Kawaguchi's force would capture Henderson Field and wipe out all the Americans east of the Lunga, while Nasu's command would advance further north, back towards the sea. When Henderson Field had been captured, the codeword *Banzai* would be radioed to Hyakutake. The whole operation would be backed by Major-General Tadashi Sumiyoshi, commander of the artillery of the Seventeenth Army, who would be responsible for putting down a heavy field of fire in the Lunga area and for making a diversionary attack from the west bank of the Matanikau River. Sumiyoshi's force would consist of five infantry battalions, a total of almost 3,000 men; a tank company, fifteen 150mm howitzers, three 100mm guns and seven field artillery pieces. The 16th Infantry would be held in reserve until Henderson Field had been taken. There would be substantial air support and Admiral Yamamoto, Commander-in-Chief of the Japanese Combined Fleet, had promised to send a carrier force under Admiral Kondo to sink any American naval vessels off the shores of Guadalcanal.

With his plans laid, Hyakutake started to execute them. His engineers began to hack a road through the jungle from Kokumbona to a point south of Henderson Field near the American perimeter. Fifteen miles long and known as the Maruyama Trail it was to run south from Kokumbona, turn east across the Matanikau and Lunga Rivers below Mount Austen, twist north and follow the Lunga, and end near the ridge above Henderson Field. Creating this trail was a work for giants. The jungle was almost impenetrable and the rain a constant factor, causing the ground underfoot to be swampy and the humidity to rise to almost unbearable proportions. Nevertheless the engineers accomplished the task so successfully that on 16th October Maruyama was able to begin his laborious march towards the airstrip. This was another

Left: Japanese tanks litter the mouth of the River Matanikau after being destroyed by US artillery fire on 23rd October. *Above:* Admiral Kondo

almost fantastic achievement. From the outset his troops were on half-rations of rice and for the entire march the torrential downpour hardly stopped. In addition to his full kit, each soldier also carried one artillery shell. The heavy guns had to be pulled through the jungle by ropes. Thousands of troops inched their way through the undergrowth at a rate of six miles a day for five days. The heavier artillery pieces had to be abandoned along the way but the men themselves got through, a tribute to their spirit. The advance had been painfully slow, however, and the original date for the attack – 18th October – had to be postponed until 22nd October. Nevertheless an entire army had been moved in secrecy to a point perilously near the American lines.

The first action of the campaign when it occurred was centred around the Matanikau River. This was on 20th October. A powerful combat patrol from General Sumiyoshi's command, including several tanks, emerged from the jungle on the west bank of the river. The patrol was seen at once from the east bank by gunners of the 3rd Battalion, 1st Marines who opened up with 37mm fire, destroying one tank and driving the remaining one and the accompanying foot soldiers back into the protective shelter of the jungle. The following day Sumiyoshi made himself felt by pumping artillery fire across the Matanikau and sending a small force of tanks and infantrymen across the sandbank at the mouth of the river. Again heavy Marine artillery fire drove the Japanese back and this put a temporary end to action in the area of the Matanikau.

Meanwhile General Maruyama's force had found the Guadalcanal jungle almost too much for them; they did not reach their position south of Henderson Field until 23rd October. Ironically, the Japanese were only slightly to the east of Bloody Ridge, the scene of their

105

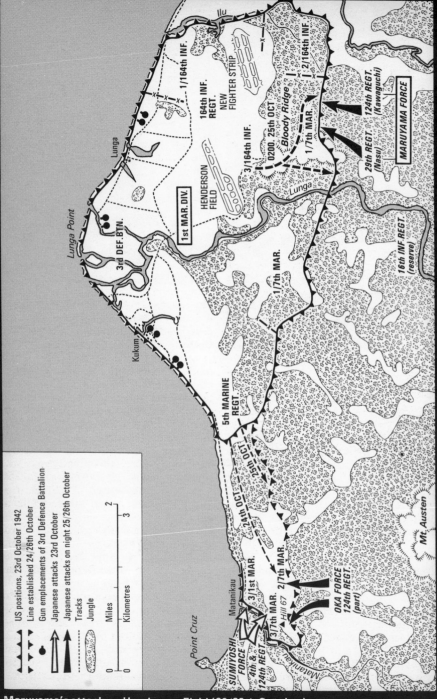

Maruyama's attack on Henderson Field (20/29th October)

Map labels:

US positions, 23rd October 1942
Line established 24/26th October
Gun emplacements of 3rd Defence Battalion
Japanese attacks 23rd October
Japanese attacks on night 25/26th October
Tracks
Jungle

Miles
Kilometres
0 — 2
0 — 3

Point Cruz
Matanikau
SUMIYOSHI FORCE
4th & 124th REGT.
3/1st MAR.
(3)7th MAR.
Hill 67
2/7th MAR.
OKA FORCE
124th REGT.
(part)
Mt. Austen

5th MARINE REGT.
24th OCT.
25th OCT.
1/7th MAR.
Kukum
3rd DEF. BTN.
Lunga Point
Lunga
Lunga
1st MAR. DIV.
HENDERSON FIELD
3/164th INF.
Lunga
1/164th INF.
164th INF. REGT.
NEW FIGHTER STRIP
Ilu
Bloody Ridge
0200. 25th OCT.
1/7th MAR.
2/164th INF.
29th REGT. (Nasu)
124th REGT. (Kawaguchi)
MARUYAMA FORCE
16th INF. REGT. (reserve)

former defeat. Even then not all the men of the expedition had reached their appointed places. A message was relayed to Maruyama that General Kawaguchi was not yet in position. Maruyama was furious; the attack, scheduled for sunset that day, would have to be postponed yet again. The general issued the necessary orders, putting the attack off for twenty-four hours. He also sent a message to Kawaguchi, relieving him of his command and turning over the latter's troops to his second-in-command, Colonel Toshinaro Shoji.

Vandegrift was not present on Guadalcanal on 23rd October. He had flown to Noumea for an urgent conference with Halsey. The man in charge on Guadalcanal for the time being was General Geiger. Geiger shared Vandegrift's belief that any Japanese attack was likely to come from the Matanikau area to the west, not the south. At sunset on 23rd October this conviction was strengthened because what seemed like a full-scale enemy attack was launched from the west.

The attack was the result of a tragic blunder. General Sumiyoshi had not been informed that the concerted attack planned for sunset on the 23rd had been postponed because of Kawaguchi's dilatory progress. Accordingly as the sun went down at about 1800 hours Sumiyoshi gave the signal for the advance across the Matanikau. Had it been part of a three-pronged attack it might have been successful, especially with air and naval artillery support. But the other units had received the radioed message to hold for twenty-four hours. Sumiyoshi's men went across the sandbank on their own. American artillery destroyed them and their tanks in a blood bath. 650 Japanese were killed in another hopeless and courageous charge.

Sumiyoshi's abortive attempt convinced General Geiger that the major Japanese advance would be made from the area of the Matanikau. He pulled one defensive battalion out of the line protecting the airfield and sent it in the direction of the Matanikau River. This meant that one American Marine battalion – Colonel Puller's – was guarding a front which was about a mile and a half long. Puller's men dug foxholes, strung wire and manhandled guns into position. At 1900 the Japanese began to infiltrate. The 29th Infantry under the command of Colonel Furumiya attempted an enveloping movement through the darkness. The Japanese moved slowly and with caution and it was not until 2300 that they unleashed the full fury of their attack through the driving rain. The 7th Company, with Furumiya at its head, actually broke through the American lines, but the marines reformed and Furumiya found himself cut off. The remainder of his command thrust itself against the marines' defences, but Puller's men held their ground, thanks to the example of such men as Sergeant John Basilone who manned a machine gun in the thick of the fray and refused to give ground even when the enemy threatened to overrun his position. Desperately Puller called for more artillery fire, and it came, but slowly his men were beginning to give ground in isolated areas. The 2nd Division, the Sendai Division, began to roll forward. Maruyama was elated, surely the Americans could not hold now. Henderson Field was sure to fall. The Japanese general prematurely released the codeword *Banzai*. It was transmitted to General Hyakutake at Kukumbona who sent it on to Rabaul. The American airstrip had been taken.

But it had not. In the small hours of the morning the battle still raged. Maruyama had even sent his reserves forward but still the Marines refused to abandon the high ground above Henderson Field. Much of the combat was now hand to hand as Americans and Japanese grappled on the slippery slopes. Geiger pushed the soldiers of the 164th Infantry up the slope to

Admiral Kinkaid

Admiral Nagumo

reinforce the marines. They turned the balance. The Japanese continued to fight until first light and then Maruyama called the remainder of his force back. Over 900 of his men lay dead on the slopes of the ridge.

The Americans had been successful again, but they wasted no time. From dawn on 25th October while the Medics collected the wounded of both sides, the survivors repaired wire and prepared for more attacks. The attacks, when they came, did not come from the land. Zeros and Bettys swooped down from Rabaul, strafing the Americans on the ridge. Wildcats took off from Henderson and gave battle in the skies above Guadalcanal. Aces like Smith (19 kills) and Carl (16 kills) had now left the Cactus Airforce for the USA but they had been replaced by men of the calibre of Captain Joseph Foss who was to register 26 kills and tie with the record previously held by Eddie Rickenbacker in the First World War, before he left Guadalcanal. Foss and the other fliers chased the Japanese aircraft back; that day Foss shot down four Zeros.

Then Japanese vessels, steaming along the Guadalcanal coast thinking that Henderson Field had been taken, thanks to Maruyama's erroneous claim, began pumping shells at the shoreline. Three enemy destroyers entered Sealark Channel from the north, drove two US destroyer-transports away and badly damaged two harbour patrol boats from Tulagi before coming under the shore-based fire of the 3rd Defence Battalion.

For the Americans trying to reorganise themselves on Guadalcanal it was a bad day. Later it became known as Dugout Sunday because of the number of times they had to take cover. There were seven separate Japanese air attacks. From 0800 to 1100 'Pistol Pete' shelled the region of Henderson Field in ten-minute bursts. While this was going on the Americans moved into new positions along the same front. During the fighting the night before; men of different units

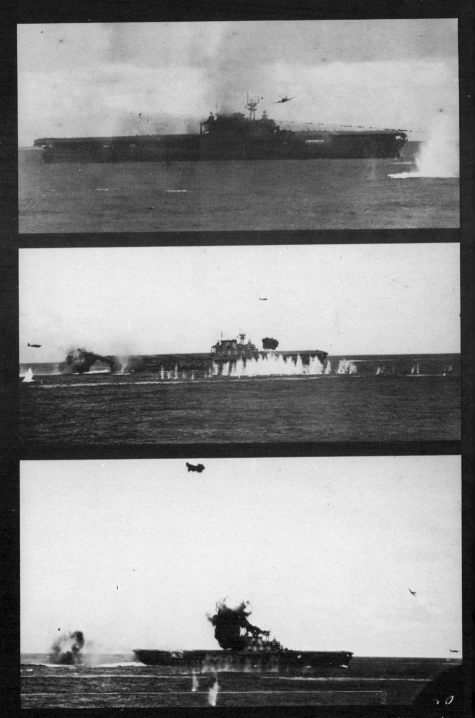

The Battle of the Santa Cruz Islands, 25th/26th October. *USS Hornet* under attack from Japanese bombers. She became the fourth US carrier to be lost in 1942

had become mixed. Now the 1st Battalion, 7th Marines occupied a line running from the Lunga River to a point almost a mile east. There the defensive position was taken up by the 3rd Battalion, 164th Infantry, which gave way farther along the line to the 2nd Battalion, 164th Infantry.

When dusk fell that evening the Japanese attacked again. There was nothing subtle about their charge. Units of 30 to 200 men hurled themselves along the length of the American line. Machine gun fire backed them up in the dark. The Japanese, men of the 16th and 29th Infantry Battalions, fought ferociously, screaming obscenities at the Americans. At approximately the same time another Japanese force charged the American line inland near the Matanikau River. This sector of the perimeter was defended by the 2nd Battalion of the 7th Marines. The Japanese broke through at one point but were driven back by a scratch force of clerks, bandsmen and specialist personnel hastily gathered together from the headquarters staff by Major Odell M Conoley, a Marine staff officer. All along the line the struggle continued. At Hill 67 Colonal Oka's force surged up the slope. Oka had not so far been noted for his willingness to join combat and his reluctance to throw in his men earlier may have cost the Japanese what chance they had of penetrating the enemy line. Now the Americans were confident and too well entrenched. Their mortars and automatic rifles scythed the Japanese down. Artillery fire tore holes in the mobs of Japanese still struggling up the incline. By dawn the Japanese had retreated down the ridge again. This time they did not come back.

For three days the Americans

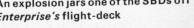

An explosion jars one of the SBDs off *Enterprise's* flight-deck

waited, the bodies of dead Japanese piled up in front of their positions. By 29th October it was obvious that the Japanese were withdrawing from the area altogether, some of the survivors going one way to Koli Point, others heading for Kokumbona. They left behind them between two and three thousand dead. American casualties had been light. The Army's 164th Infantry, for example, whose first major action on Guadalcanal this had been, lost 26 killed and 52 wounded. The Americans had fought bravely and skilfully. They had possessed the advantage of being well dug in and of possessing powerful weapons. But a major cause of the Japanese defeat had been the lack of flexibility among the Japanese command on the island. When the difficult terrain made a co-ordination of attack impossible, Hyakutake and his staff still went ahead with their frontal assault. Allied to this, the breakdown in communications and the lack of vigour of such men as Oka doomed the attack on Henderson Field to failure.

The Americans were not successful in every sphere on the night of 25th/26th October. While the land forces were repulsing the Japanese around the airfield American naval vessels were engaged in a battle of their own off the Santa Cruz islands east of Guadalcanal. Two American task forces had been in the area, one centred around the carrier *Enterprise* under Rear-Admiral Kinkaid and consisting of the battleship *South Dakota*, two cruisers and eight destroyers; and the other made up of the carrier *Hornet* commanded by Rear-Admiral Murray, and two heavy cruisers, two anti-aircraft cruisers and six destroyers. The American vessels encountered a Japanese force under Vice-Admiral

By now a fuel-drum bridge had been built over the Matanikau

Brigadier Sebree

Colonel Carlson

Nagumo comprising four carriers, four battleships, eight cruisers and about thirty destroyers. The Japanese were kept informed of the progress of the American ships by a network of submarines and aircraft. The battle, when it was joined, was another inconclusive one but the Americans suffered the loss of the *Hornet*, sunk by Japanese aircraft, and the destroyer *Porter*, torpedoed by a submarine. In addition *Enterprise* and *South Dakota* were damaged and seventy-four US planes lost. The Japanese lost one hundred aircraft while the carriers *Shokaku* and *Zuiho*, the heavy cruiser *Chikuma* and the destroyer *Terutsuki* were badly damaged.

The loss of the *Hornet* and, temporarily, of *Enterprise* and their aircraft was a blow but Vandegrift, now back on Guadalcanal, did not intend to lose the advantage he had gained over the Japanese on the island. It was essential that the retreating Japanese be followed up and their stragglers killed or captured. Also, in the Matanikau and Point Cruz areas the Japanese heavy artillery could still cause damage; a quick push might either capture 'Pistol Pete' and the other big guns or at least cause the Japanese to withdraw them. Accordingly Vandegrift mounted yet another expedition to cross the Matanikau River. He chose the 5th Marines who had missed the brunt of the recent fighting, the 1st and 2nd Battalions of the 2nd Marines previously stationed on Tulagi, the 3rd Battalion, 7th Marines, Whaling's scout-snipers, and an artillery battalion in support.

On the night of 31st October engineers of the 1st Engineer Battalion (A, C and D Companies) threw three bridges across the Matanikau and the advance began as scheduled early on the morning of 1st November. The Americans fanned out and advanced on the west bank of the Matanikau. The 1st Battalion, 5th Marines encountered some opposition in the region of Point Cruz, but by the end of the day the 2nd Battalion, 5th

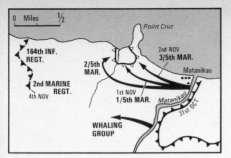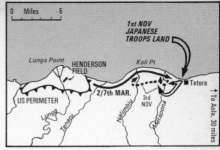

The drive to Kokumbuna is frustrated by Japanese landings east of Lunga Point

Marines had moved well ahead on the left of the advancing line. The following morning, 2nd November, the reserve 3rd Battalion of the 5th Marines moved forward to help the 1st Battalion; at the same time the 2nd Battalion wheeled round to surround the Japanese confronting the other two battalions. By 3rd November this had been accomplished. The Japanese were surrounded on three sides by marines and on the fourth by the sea. Three successive bayonet charges put paid to the Japanese.

The advance was going well, and on the 4th of November Whaling's scout-snipers and the 5th Marines were replaced by the 2nd Marines and the 164th Infantry Regiment. Then, due to no fault of their own, the Americans west of the Matanikau had to stop their progress. It was reported that there had been fresh Japanese landings to the east of the American perimeter. Some of the Americans west of the Matanikau were ordered to dig in, the rest were pulled back to face the new threat.

The landings had been observed by Lieutenant-Colonel Hanneken and his men of the 2nd Battalion, 7th Marines. On 1st November the battalion had headed east, making for the vicinity of Koli Point. The following day the marines reached the Metapona River and waited until dusk before crossing it. Hanneken then advanced about a mile further east and settled in along a line on the beach, running back as far as the Metapona River. It was

then that the marines saw the Japanese unloading in the region of Tetere. There had been heavy rain that day and the radio transmitters belonging to the battalion were out of action and Hanneken had been unable to report back to the perimeter.

At dawn the following morning, 3rd November, a Japanese patrol stumbled across the American line. The marines opened fire, killing four Japanese, but four others escaped. Further concealment was impossible so Hanneken called down heavy mortar fire upon the Japanese unloading parties on the beach. As the morning wore on the colonel decided to risk an attack. Before he could give the order the Japanese directed heavy artillery fire upon his position from guns unloaded from the ships off the shore. After the fire had stopped several hundred Japanese soldiers charged at the Americans along the beach. Hanneken decided not to attack and ordered his men to pull back to the river and to cross it if possible. This manoeuvre was carried out successfully by mid-afternoon, but no sooner had Hanneken withdrawn to the west bank of the Metapona than he was attacked from the rear by another Japanese force. Hanneken kept his head and managed to pass a message back to headquarters. He then left one company to fight off the Japanese attack which was coming from inland, and began to pull back towards the safety of the American perimeter.

As soon as Hanneken's message was

115

received, which was at about 1445 on 3rd November, Vandegrift set about organising reinforcements. He ordered the 1st Battalion, 7th Marines (Lieutenant Colonel Puller), the 3rd Battalion of the 164th Infantry, Whaling's scout-snipers and a battalion of the 10th Marines artillery, which had not long arrived on Guadalcanal, to proceed east and help Hanneken. Initially Rupertus was intended to command this force but he fell ill and was replaced by Army Brigadier E B Sebree, ADC of the Americal Division. Such a large force could not move quickly and it was 6th November before it had made contact with the Japanese and 10th November before Sebree felt in a position to order an attack. When the attack was made it was successful. The Japanese were trapped between Hanneken's battalion and Puller's battalion at Gavaga Creek. Over 350 Japanese were killed but a much larger force under Colonel Shoji broke through the lines of the 164th Infantry which had been attempting a flanking movement, and escaped inland, leaving behind them a number of artillery pieces, some landing boats and fifteen tons of rice. Forty Americans were killed and 120 wounded in this action.

The Japanese who escaped through the lines of the 164th Infantry were pursued by men of Lieutenant Colonel Evans F Carlson's 2nd Raider Battalion. Carlson's force had been in the area largely thanks to Admiral Turner's conviction that American forces should be dispersed along the coast of Guadalcanal for mopping up operations. Turner had persuaded a reluctant Vandegrift to build a new airstrip at Aola, thirty miles from the American perimeter on the northeast coast of Guadalcanal. Vandegrift's engineers had protested about the unsuitability of this site, pointing out that the terrain was too rough for an airstrip, but the admiral had prevailed. It later turned out that the engineers had been right, and the project was abandoned. Before that,

however, a force had been landed at Aola consisting of a Naval Construction Battalion and the 5th Defence Battalion. To protect this combination the 147th Infantry had been brought from Tonga, while the initial landing was made by C and E Battalions of Carlson's Raiders, lately in the New Hebrides. Carlson had served in China and had adopted the slogan 'Gung Ho!' ('Work Together') for his Raiders.

The Aola landing had been made without opposition early in November. Later in the month the Seabees were to be ordered to abandon their work, but at the time that the Japanese were eluding the 164th Infantry it meant that the Raiders were in a position to intercept them. This was a task after Carlson's own heart. Between 11th and 18th November the Raiders fought a series of running battles with Shoji's men. The Japanese retreated further inland. The Raiders

went after them, living off the land, seldom bothering to report their progress to headquarters, and fighting what was in effect a private war with the enemy. Carlson's exploits are summed up in the official Division Report on the Raiders: 'In exactly thirty days the Raiders had executed a long and arduous transit of mountains and forbidding country. They had fought no less than twelve successful actions and had counted enemy dead in excess of four hundred.'

It was 4th December before Carlson and his Raiders returned. They had lost seventeen men. Throughout their action they had relied to a great extent on Solomon Islanders as bearers and guides. Throughout the campaign on Guadalcanal the islanders continued to be of the utmost service to the Allies. Acting as scouts and guides, making up labour gangs, rescuing isolated soldiers and crashed

Colonel Carlson's Raiders land at Aola, on the eastern end of Guadalcanal, in early November

fliers, the Solomon Islanders were loyal to the Allied cause. Perhaps if the Japanese had behaved with more tact and consideration they might have received more help from the Melanesians, but after an initial attempt to ingratiate themselves the Japanese made little effort to enlist the sympathies of the natives. Japanese soldiers looted gardens, pressed islanders into service without paying them and generally treated them as if they were of no account. In their turn the inhabitants of Guadalcanal did everything they could to hinder the Japanese, from withholding information to attacking detached patrols.

Offensive

On 8th November Admiral Halsey visited Guadalcanal. His stay, though brief, was as usual colourful. General Vandegrift took him on a tour of the perimeter area, pointing out some of the now famous battlefields. That night 'Washing Machine Charlie' made one of its visits. Halsey and Vandegrift took shelter in the latter's dugout. The admiral looked with approval at the barricade of sandbags around them. 'Stout structure you have here,' he said, punching one of the bags. The rotten canvas burst and the sand poured out. The next morning at a press conference the Commander South Pacific Area was in confident form. He was asked how long he thought the Japanese would continue fighting. 'How long can they take it?' retorted the admiral. Another correspondent asked Halsey how he planned to win the campaign. 'Kill Japs, kill Japs, and keep on killing Japs,' said Halsey.

Then Halsey left Guadalcanal, informing Vandegrift that a major convoy was on its way carrying the Army 182nd Infantry. This was good news but there was still plenty of work on hand for the Marine commander. Reinforcements, including the 8th Marines, were now coming in in increasing numbers, but the Japanese were strengthening their position as well. Between 2nd and 10th November the Tokyo Express brought sixty-five destroyers to Guadalcanal, all unloading men and supplies.

On 10th November Vandegrift considered that the situation to the east of the perimeter was now well in hand and that he could order the advance west of the Matanikau to be resumed. Again the advance was cut short. This time a message had been received from a coastwatcher in the Buin-Faisi area on Bougainville in the Western Solomons. A large Japanese naval force was massing there. The coastwatcher reported 61 ships, including 6 cruisers and 33 destroyers. American intelligence was sure that the Japanese were planning an all-out attack on Guadalcanal.

This is just what they were doing. Hyakutake had decided to reinforce the Japanese on Guadalcanal (now some 30,000 men) with 11,000 men of the 38th Division under Lieutenant-General Tadayoshi Sano, and 3,000 men of a naval landing force. The plans for landing this combined force were straightforward. A section of the 2nd Fleet would be sent under Vice-Admiral Hiroaki Abe, consisting of the battleships *Hiei* and *Kirishima*, the cruiser *Nagara* and fourteen destroyers. This force would do its

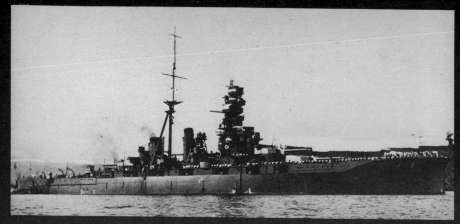

The Japanese battleship *Hiei,* crippled at Guadalcanal

USS Atlanta, Admiral Scott's flagship at Guadalcanal

USS Washington, which sunk the Japanese battleship *Kirishima*

best to destroy Henderson Field with an intensive bombardment from off the shore. Admiral Kondo would take the rest of his 2nd Fleet, including the aircraft carriers *Junyo* and *Hiyo*, the battleships *Kongo* and *Haruna*, four cruisers and nineteen destroyers to a point about 150 miles north of the island of Savo, from which position its aircraft, almost one hundred in number could be dispatched. While these back-up activities were going on, Vice Admiral Mikawa and a force of six cruisers and six destroyers of his 8th Fleet would support the landing of Sano's 38th Division in the area of Tassafaronga. The troops would travel in eleven transports escorted by twelve destroyers under Rear-Admiral Tanaka. For the first time in the Guadalcanal operation the Japanese were sending a massive force 'all at once, in big ships' as Admiral Mikawa had been urging for months. The landing was scheduled for 2200 on 13th November.

With the Japanese bringing their naval force down from Rabaul, and Halsey sending a major task force of 6 cruisers, 14 destroyers, 4 transports and 3 cargo ships from Noumea and Espiritu Santo to rendezvous off the coast of San Cristobal on the morning of 11th November, it meant that two large opposing naval forces were in the vicinity of Guadalcanal at the same time. Halsey also had another force in reserve at Noumea comprising 2 battleships, 2 cruisers, 8 destroyers and the only partially repaired carrier *Enterprise*. *Enterprise* was the only United States aircraft carrier in the South Pacific.

A task force under Rear-Admiral Scott reached Lunga Point on 11th November. The following day it was joined by Turner with *Portland*, four destroyers and four transports carrying the men of the 182nd Infantry. Turner had rendezvoused as planned the previous day off San Cristobal with the force under Rear-Admiral Callaghan before proceeding to Kukum to unload the troops. The

Rear Admiral Daniel J Callaghan

Rear Admiral Willis A Lee

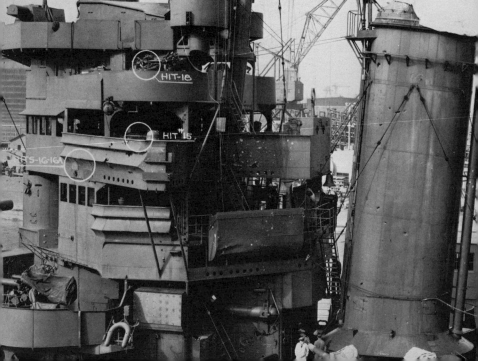

US transports under attack from the air, off Lunga Point, 11th November

ships at anchor were attacked by twenty-five Japanese torpedo planes escorted by eight Zero fighters. One Japanese aircraft crashed into the after control station of the cruiser *San Francisco*, killing thirty men. The destroyer *Buchanan* was also damaged but by American anti-aircraft fire. The same morning Turner received word that a force under Admiral Abe had been seen apparently making for Henderson Field. Turner at once ordered Admiral Callaghan to intercept this force and protect Henderson Field.

The resulting Naval Battle of Guadalcanal has been respectively described by an American commander (Admiral Turner) as 'the fiercest naval battle ever fought' and by a Japanese present (Captain Tameichi Hara) as 'one of the most fantastic sea-battles of modern history in that it was fought at almost point-blank range between fourteen Japanese and thirteen American warships.'

Rear-Admiral Callaghan knew that the enemy had larger ships and bigger guns and that his best chance of success would be to surprise the Japanese and attack them before they were ready. Vice-Admiral Abe guessed that these would be the American tactics and so drew his vessels into a very tight formation. Both admirals were later criticised: Abe for his ultra-caution and Callaghan for failing to lay down a comprehensive battle plan. The battle began at 0124 on 13th November. It took place between Guadalcanal and the island of Savo. Previously Abe had been advancing through a rain squall but now the weather had cleared, although the night was very dark. Suddenly *Helena* picked up the Japanese bombardment force on her radar at 27,000 yards

San Francisco, back in a California dockyard, bears the marks of the damage she suffered during the battle

123

distance. The information was at once passed to Callaghan. The American knew that he was in a very dangerous situation. Not only were his vessels outgunned by those of Abe, but his most effective radar was on another ship, and the land mass of Guadalcanal made it difficult to get a correct radar reading. To add to Callaghan's difficulties communications between the ships of his force were bad. The admiral was not even sure that the ships reported were Japanese. Twenty-four minutes passed before he gave the order to open fire. In that time the Americans had lost most of the advantage of surprise. Callaghan sailed between two columns of Japanese ships and opened fire at a distance of 3,000 yards. At the same time the Japanese saw the American vessels and opened fire in their turn. In the darkness it was almost impossible to tell friend from foe and the confusion was indescribable as the warships pumped shells and torpedoes at each other at an ever-decreasing range. The commanders of the two forces could not control the overall action and the captain of each ship set his own course and chose his own foes.

Rear Admiral Scott had been detailed to join Callaghan's command. His flagship *Atlanta* was one of the first to be crippled and Scott was killed. Couragously two destroyers, *Cushing* and *Laffey* went for the Japanese battleship *Hiei*, their guns blazing. The *Laffey* scored a number of hits and then *Hiei* got its range and that of *Cushing*, damaging the former and sinking the latter. More American destroyers closed in on the Japanese battleship. *Hiei* began to pull out of distance, crippled. Other Japanese ships fought on tenaciously. *San Francisco* was badly damaged and Callaghan and most of his officers killed. *Portland* was badly damaged. Out of eight US destroyers, four were

sunk and three damaged. Another casualty was *Juneau*, sunk the following morning by the Japanese submarine I-26. 700 men, all but ten of the crew, were killed including five brothers, the Sullivans.

Japanese casualties were less severe. Two destroyers were sunk and the battlship *Hiei* so badly crippled that the following day she was caught by aircraft from Henderson Field and the carrier *Enterprise*. The planes inflicted more damage on *Hiei* and the Japanese scuttled her, the first Japanese battleship to be lost in the war. Admiral Abe and the battleship's captain Masao Nishida were taken off on the *Yukikaze*. Both men were later relieved of their commands by an irate Japanese High Command. The Americans had won the Battle of Guadalcanal because Abe had withdrawn without bombarding Henderson Field. But the victory had been achieved at a staggering cost. Of all the US vessels taking part in the battle, only *Fletcher* escaped unscathed. Five ships had been sunk, eight badly damaged and 700 officers and men killed, including two admirals. No country could afford too many victories of this nature.

There were still many combat vessels in the Guadalcanal area. Admiral Tanaka had obeyed orders to withdraw his transports to the safety of the Shortlands temporarily, but Admiral Mikawa was heading for Henderson Field to achieve what Abe had failed to do. On the night of 13th/14th November he took three cruisers and four destroyers along the Guadalcanal coast and fired over a thousand 8-inch shells at Henderson Field and two adjacent airstrips. The bombardment lasted for forty-five minutes and might have gone on longer had it not been for the efforts of some American torpedo boats which sallied out of Tulagi harbour and launched torpedoes at the enemy cruisers, driving them off.

This attack, coming so soon after Callaghan's force had repulsed Abe's

One of Tanaka's beached transports silhouetted against the Pacific skyline

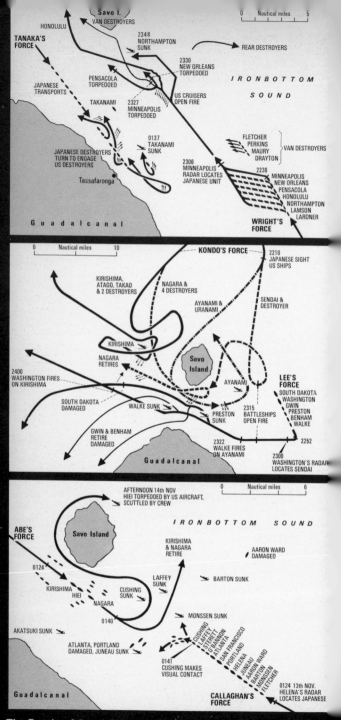

Map 1 (top):

Savo I.
VAN DESTROYERS
HONOLULU

TANAKA'S FORCE

2348 NORTHAMPTON SUNK

REAR DESTROYERS

0   Nautical miles   5

2330 NEW ORLEANS TORPEDOED

JAPANESE TRANSPORTS

PENSACOLA TORPEDOED

TAKANAMI

2327 MINNEAPOLIS TORPEDOED

US CRUISERS OPEN FIRE

I R O N B O T T O M

S O U N D

0137 TAKANAMI SUNK

FLETCHER
PERKINS
MAURY
DRAYTON

} VAN DESTROYERS

JAPANESE DESTROYERS TURN TO ENGAGE US DESTROYERS

Tassafaronga

2306 MINNEAPOLIS RADAR LOCATES JAPANESE UNIT

2238

MINNEAPOLIS
NEW ORLEANS
PENSACOLA
HONOLULU
NORTHAMPTON
LAMSON
LARDNER

G u a d a l c a n a l

WRIGHT'S FORCE

Map 2 (middle):

0   Nautical miles   10

KONDO'S FORCE

2210 JAPANESE SIGHT US SHIPS

KIRISHIMA, ATAGO, TAKAO & 2 DESTROYERS

NAGARA & 4 DESTROYERS

AYANAMI & URANAMI

SENDAI & DESTROYER

KIRISHIMA

Savo Island

NAGARA RETIRES

AYANAMI

LEE'S FORCE

SOUTH DAKOTA
WASHINGTON
GWIN
PRESTON
BENHAM
WALKE

2400 WASHINGTON FIRES ON KIRISHIMA

SOUTH DAKOTA DAMAGED

WALKE SUNK

PRESTON SUNK

2315 BATTLESHIPS OPEN FIRE

GWIN & BENHAM RETIRE DAMAGED

2252

G u a d a l c a n a l

2322 WALKE FIRES ON AYANAMI

2300 WASHINGTON'S RADAR LOCATES SENDAI

Map 3 (bottom):

AFTERNOON 14th NOV
HIEI TORPEDOED BY US AIRCRAFT, SCUTTLED BY CREW

0   Nautical miles   6

ABE'S FORCE

Savo Island

I R O N B O T T O M   S O U N D

KIRISHIMA & NAGARA RETIRE

AARON WARD DAMAGED

0124

KIRISHIMA

HIEI

LAFFEY SUNK

BARTON SUNK

CUSHING SUNK

NAGARA

0140

MONSSEN SUNK

AKATSUKI SUNK

ATLANTA, PORTLAND DAMAGED, JUNEAU SUNK

CUSHING
LAFFEY
STERETT
O'BANNON
ATLANTA
SAN FRANCISCO
PORTLAND
HELENA
JUNEAU
AARON WARD
BARTON
MONSSEN
FLETCHER

0141 CUSHING MAKES VISUAL CONTACT

0124 13th NOV. HELENA'S RADAR LOCATES JAPANESE

G u a d a l c a n a l

CALLAGHAN'S FORCE

The Battle of Guadalcanal, night, 14/15th November 1942
The Battle of Tassafaronga, 30th November 1942
The Battle of Guadalcanal, early morning, 13th November 194

attack towards Henderson, was a blow to the Americans who had thought the airfield safe for a while. Luckily the bombardment had not put the strip out of action. At dawn on 14th November a number of aircraft took off from the airfield and went looking for the bombardment force. They caught up with Mikawa, damaging a number of his vessels and slowing *Kinugasa* sufficiently for aircraft from *Enterprise* to finish her off later that day. Mikawa had to head for the shelter of the Shortlands and was unable to provide an escort for Tanaka's transports and destroyers which were now proceeding to their delayed landing on Guadalcanal. Admiral Kondo sent air cover but in insufficient numbers. Tanaka's troopships were an open target for aeroplanes from Henderson Field and from the carrier *Enterprise*. Five times between noon and sunset airstrikes hit the transports. From the New Hebrides B-17s were sent to add to the slaughter. Six of the eleven transports were sunk and a seventh badly damaged and sent back to the Shortlands. By dusk only four transports were still heading for Guadalcanal.

Admiral Kondo had seen three days of near disaster. Now he headed for Guadalcanal himself in order to put Henderson Field out of action once and for all. He took with him the battleship *Kirishima*, the cruisers *Atago*, *Takao*, *Sendai* and *Nagara*, and nine destroyers. Rear-Admiral Willis Lee was sent towards Savo to head the Japanese off. Lee commanded *Washington* and *South Dakota* with a screen of four destroyers. Lee reached Ironbottom Bay between Savo and Guadalcanal and cruised up and down in the darkness, waiting for Kondo. At 2315 he made contact by radar with the Japanese. At once *Washington* and *South Dakota* opened fire. The Japanese were taken by surprise but soon recovered. Torpedoes sunk the American destroyers *Preston*, *Benham* and *Walke* or so badly disabled them that they were unable to continue the

fight. The Japanese also raked *South Dakota*, crippling her and forcing her to withdraw. Lee in *Washington* was more successful. His big guns shattered *Kirishima* so that she later sank, and so badly hammered the cruisers that the Japanese turned and fled, leaving Lee in command of Ironbottom Bay.

Meanwhile Tanaka and his four remaining transports were approaching Guadalcanal. Realising that he could expect no help from Kondo and that Lee was probably searching for him Tanaka appealed for permission to run his transports aground and beach them. Admiral Kondo gave the necessary permission and at dawn on 15th November Tanaka sent the transports on to the beach at Tassafaronga before hastily withdrawing with his destroyer escorts. American artillery shelled the beached craft and the soldiers scuttling ashore, while aircraft swooped in on strafing expeditions. That 2,000 Japanese troops managed to escape into the shelter of the jungle is a tribute to their agility and presence of mind under fire.

The four-day Battle of Guadalcanal was over. Heavy losses had been incurred on both sides but the Japanese had definitely been beaten off. It was a turning point, perhaps the most significant so far. Writing of it afterwards Halsey was to say, 'If our ships and planes had been routed in this battle, if we had lost it our troops on Guadalcanal would have been trapped as were our troops on Bataan . . . Unobstructed, the enemy would have driven south, at our supply lines to New Zealand and Australia and enveloped them.' Captain Hara, who had been present almost throughout, was scathing of his own leaders, particularly of Kondo and his flight from Lee off Guadalcanal: 'Many of Kondo's officers were ashamed of him and of themselves. They preferred not to talk about the battle.'

The Japanese continued to claim the Battle of Guadalcanal as a victory

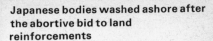

Japanese bodies washed ashore after
the abortive bid to land
reinforcements

which, in terms of enemy ships destroyed, it was. But the High Command knew that the American morale had reached a fresh height. General Vandegrift, in a message to Halsey, said 'We believe the enemy has suffered a crushing defeat. We thank Lee for his sturdy effort of last night.' At a news conference in Washington on 16th November, Secretary Knox declared jubilantly 'We can lick them. I don't qualify that. We'll defeat them.' His remarks were echoed at Nouméa by Halsey: 'We've got the bastards licked.'

In Japan it was a time for rethinking and recrimination. After the war, Captain Ohmae, in charge of naval planning at Rabaul, summed up the inter-service bickering when he complained 'The navy lost ships, aeroplanes and pilots while trying to give support to the land assault which was continually delayed. The army did not understand the position of the navy in that it could not stay in one area indefinitely without being attacked. We were also consuming valuable fuel.' Ohmae was referring to one particular action but his words could apply to the general controversy between the two services. The Japanese were also beginning to suffer from a lack of air support, which in turn was due to insufficient air bases. Masatake Okumiya, a Japanese air commander engaged in the Guadalcanal operations was to write: 'There is little question that had our air combat forces received adequate support through construction of new air bases and the proper maintenance of existing facilities, we could have destroyed many more enemy planes and ships, and might have influenced the ground fighting in our favour. However, the situation deteriorated steadily as Japanese con-

A camp on Guadalcanal

129

struction crews seemingly delayed endlessly their efforts to build new air bases.'

By November the American production of war materials was getting into its swing and the forces on Guadalcanal of the US Command were certainly better equipped than were the Japanese. The Americans, too, were ahead of the Japanese in such refinements as radar-controlled naval gunfire. In the air, too, the Japanese who had at first possessed in the Zero the most capable aircraft in the Pacific theatre were to be outstripped by the Americans with their Boeing B-17 Flying Fortresses and the P-38s. The B-17, with its radius in excess of 750 nautical miles and its self-sealing fuel tanks and the protection afforded by its 12.7mm machine guns made it a most formidable heavy bomber, able to penetrate clouds of Zero fighters. The P-38, able to patrol at great speeds at high altitudes, was another excellent aircraft.

But although the Japanese had been repelled once at sea and despite the fact that their Zeros no longer controlled the skies above Guadalcanal, they had one great ability both on land, in the air and at sea – the courage and fighting skill of many of their men. This was to be borne home to the Americans on several occasions before the end of November.

Almost before the Battle of Guadalcanal was over Vandegrift was planning his next move on land. This was to advance further west from the Matanikau area to the Poha River and dig in there. A large force consisting of most of the 182nd Infantry, the 164th Infantry, the 8th Marines, and a reserve of the 1st Marines, all under the command of Brigadier-General Sebree was deputed to advance against the remainder of Hyakutake's force. There had been reorganisations at top level in the Japanese command,

with Lieutenant-General Hitoshi Imamura as the commander of Eighth Area Army. Hyakutake, however, had retained command of the Seventh Army on Guadalcanal, with instructions to recapture Guadalcanal. By this time Hyakutake and his men had few illusions about their capabilities. They were hungry and disease-ridden. Even the Americans were reporting malaria victims in excess of 2,000 a month; the Japanese were in a worse state. There would be little hope of advancing in their present condition without sufficient air cover. They could still defend, however, and would do so against any American advance.

On 18th November Sebree's force headed towards Point Cruz. By 20th November the 182nd Infantry had dug in about a hundred yards east of Point Cruz. The Japanese attacked at dawn. The Americans gave ground before the determined enemy charge. They were rallied by their officers and went forward again, only to be halted by Japanese mortar and artillery fire. Sebree brought up the 164th Infantry but the Japanese were fighting superbly and the Americans could make no progress. The situation was getting desperate and Sebree ordered his troops to withdraw 300 yards while artillery shelled the area for half an hour. When the thirty minutes barrage had ended Sebree sent the 8th Marines forward. The marines made no more impression on the Japanese than the army had done. Vandegrift took in the situation and sent his orders to Sebree. The Americans were to dig in where they were. There was obviously going to be no easy advance to the Poha and beyond.

There were going to be no easy mopping-up operations at sea either, not as long as the Japanese had admirals of the calibre of Tanaka. The latter had been entrusted with the task of landing supplies to the Japanese troops on Guadalcanal. It was no longer possible to approach the coast with impunity so a new system had been devised. This consisted of loading the supplies into drums which were then dropped over the side of destroyers at night in the hope that they would drift ashore. On 27th November Tanaka left Rabaul on one of these night missions. By the early morning of 30th November the destroyers were heading for Guadalcanal. A spotter craft sighted the destroyer force and Tanaka issued the following message to his vessels: 'It is probable that we will encounter the enemy tonight. Although our primary mission is to land supplies, everyone is to be ready for combat. If an engagement occurs, take the initiative and destroy the enemy.'

By 2100 Tanaka and his eight destroyers were off the coast at Tassafaronga. An American force under Rear-Admiral Wright had been sent from Espiritu Santo in the New Hebrides to attack Tanaka. A few minutes after 2100 some of Wright's ships picked up the Japanese vessels on their radar screens and at once fired torpedoes at them. They all missed. *Takanami*, however, was hit and sunk by gunfire from the American vessels. At 2122 Tanaka, having summed up the situation, ordered 'All ships, full battle speed.' He swung his destroyers round so that they were approaching the Americans from the side, and gave the order to release torpedoes. The salvo was devastatingly effective. Four American cruisers, *Minneapolis, Pensacola, New Orleans* and *Northampton* were badly damaged, the last named so badly that she sank. In a contest between Japanese destroyers and American cruisers Tanaka had brought off a convincing victory. Not one of his destroyers was hit in the action except *Takanami*. He withdrew without landing his cargo, which caused great displeasure at Rabaul, but he had scored a significant victory over a superior force.

The Americans were angry and humiliated by Wright's failure to defeat Tanaka, but they were not unduly dismayed. Things were going too well for that. At the beginning

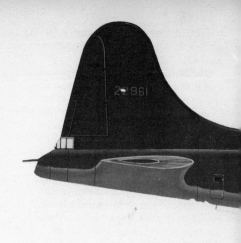

The Boeing B-17 was a standard bomber with the United States Air Force throughout the war, and was continually modified to keep it abreast of the latest combat conditions. The model illustrated is a B-17F. *Engines:* Four Wright R-1820 -97 radials, 1,200 hp. *Armament:* Twelve .5-inch machine guns plus up to 20,800 pounds of bombs for very short ranges, through normal maximum bomb load was 12,800 pounds. *Maximum speed:* 299 mph at 25,000 feet. *Climb:* 25.7 minutes to 20,000 feet. *Ceiling:* 37,500 feet. *Range:* 1,300 miles with 6,000 pounds of bombs. *Weights empty/loaded:* 34,000 /56,500 pounds. *Span:* 103 feet 9 inches. *Length:* 74 feet 9 inches

of December the 1st Marines and General Vandegrift left Guadalcanal, the latter to be replaced by Major-General Patch. On 7th December Vandegrift wrote a letter to the men who had fought under him, giving his thanks to 'the soldiers and marines who have faced the enemy in the fierceness of night combat, to the pilots, army, navy and marines, whose unbelievable achievements have made the name 'Guadalcanal' a synonym for death and disaster in the language

A New Hebrides based B-17 on a bombing sortie over Gizo Island

General Patch

Rear Admiral Wright

of our enemy; to those who have laboured and sweated within the lines at all manner of prodigious and vital tasks; to the men of the torpedo boat command slashing at the enemy in night sorties; to our small band of devoted allies who have contributed so vastly in proportion to their numbers; to the surface forces of the navy associated with us in signal triumphs of their own...'

Medical examinations revealed that a third of the marines leaving Guadalcanal were unfit for combat duty. Some of them were unable to climb the netting leading to the decks of the ships which were taking them away.

Major-General Alexander Patch had formerly commanded the Americal Division in New Caledonia. When he took over on Guadalcanal he discovered that many of his troops were in almost as bad condition as Vandegrift's evacuated marines. He therefore decided not to advance until fresh troops were delivered to the theatre of operations. Patch took the attitude, rightly as it turned out, that he could afford to wait; the Japanese, short of food and medical supplies, could not. Any activity, Patch decided, would be strictly local until January.

The first local action took place in the area of Mount Austen near the original site of the American landing at Red Beach. It was not a successful one. On 17th December the 3rd Battalion, 132nd Infantry made an attempt to storm the Japanese position, assisted by two companies of the 1st Battalion. For four days the Americans tried to advance but the Japanese had the advantage of the slope and were well entrenched. On 22nd December the Americans withdrew while their artillery plastered the mountainside and aircraft strafed the area. Then the troops advanced to their previous position and stayed there. On 27th December an attempt was

Relieved after months of fighting, weary Marines return from the front

made to advance but again the Japanese would not be budged from their position and continued to rain fire down upon any Americans who appeared. On 31st December reinforcements arrived in the shape of the 2nd Battalion, 132nd Infantry. Still the badly managed engagement dragged on. The Americans suffered 182 casualties and their commander requested that he be relieved of his command. It was not until January that the Americans took Mount Austen, and by that time the Japanese were in general retreat.

From the Western Solomons Admiral Tanaka was still running his celebrated Tokyo Express down to Guadalcanal to float supplies ashore to the Japanese troops sticking it out in the jungle. On 3rd December he succeeded in delivering 1,500 drums of supplies, unopposed by American naval forces. US aircraft attacked his vessels, however, and only 500 of the drums ended up in Japanese hands. On 7th December Tanaka made another run; this time he ran into American aircraft and torpedo boats and was driven away. He returned

four nights later on 11th December and dropped 1,200 drums over the side, but only about 200 reached the stranded Japanese. In addition Tanaka lost his flagship, *Teruzuki*, torpedoed by torpedo boats, and had to transfer to another vessel in order to make his escape. Tanaka was injured in this raid and was taken to a hospital in Rabaul. Upon his release he was transferred to Singapore.

Also in December the Allies received rather more welcome visitors than Tanaka and the Tokyo Express. These were the Fijians. The first of these

The Americal Division on Red Beach

troops to arrive were thirty Commandos, a 'specimen party' sent to see if they fitted in with the American troops. They did this with a vengeance and became the most popular as well as some of the most effective soldiers on the island. The Fijians excelled in patrol work behind the enemy lines and before long many more had joined the original thirty. A detachment of Tongans also reached Guadalcanal, but were to do most of their work in the Western Solomons.

Evacuation

The Japanese army and navy had been unable successfully to integrate their attacks. Japan did not possess the resources to match those of the USA in a long drawn-out war. Her armed forces were spread too thin and too wide. On 4th January, 1943, Imperial Headquarters issued the order for all Japanese troops to be withdrawn from Guadalcanal. It was emphasised that this was purely a local withdrawal; the campaign in New Guinea would continue.

The Japanese military commanders responsible for the Guadalcanal campaign were reluctant to break off the fighting there. The Commander of the EighthArmy was forced to bow to the wishes of Tokyo, as was the Senior Naval Commander at Rabaul, Vice-Admiral Jinichi Kusaka. The machinery needed to conduct the withdrawal began to get under way. although the troops fighting on the island were not informed of the situation.

The Americans, too, had no idea that the Japanese were planning to move off Guadalcanal. Cautiously General Patch continued to wait until he was sure that he was at full strength. He wanted to be absolutely sure that when he did move everything had been planned down to the last detail. Patch was fortunate in that he could learn from the mistakes of the first marines to land on the island, and because he inherited four or five months accumulated wisdom and experience bequeathed him by Vandegrift and his staff. By the end of 1942 the Americans had a pretty good idea of what would work and what would not against the Japanese on Guadalcanal.

Tactically, for example, it had been proved that after a beachhead landing it was better to advance in columns on a broad front, but that when it came to penetrating the jungle the most suitable formation was to march in column of files. It had also been

The Japanese decision to withdraw from Guadalcanal was agreed to by the Emperor on 31st December, 1942, but the Japanese High Command had made up its mind to abandon the island some time before. The tide of the war was slowly turning against the Japanese, indeed the tenacious American stand on Guadalcanal had done a great deal to turn it, showing that the Japanese were not supermen and that they did not possess a monopoly of fighting spirit. Many Japanese military reputations had been tarnished on and around the island. The Japanese air strength had exhausted itself against the planes and pilots of Henderson Field and the navy carriers.

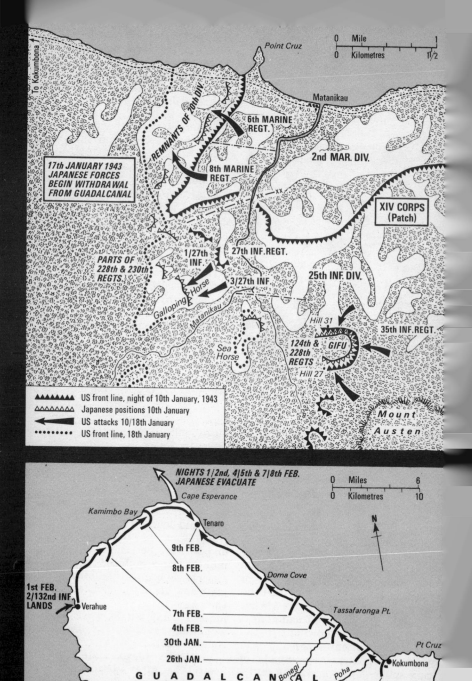

Top map:

To Kokumbona

Point Cruz

0 Mile 1
0 Kilometres 1 1/2

Matanikau

REMNANTS OF 20th DIV.

6th MARINE REGT.

2nd MAR. DIV.

17th JANUARY 1943 JAPANESE FORCES BEGIN WITHDRAWAL FROM GUADALCANAL

8th MARINE REGT

XIV CORPS (Patch)

PARTS OF 228th & 230th REGTS.

1/27th INF.

27th INF.REGT.

Galloping Horse

3/27th INF

25th INF. DIV.

Matanikau

Hill 31

35th INF. REGT.

Sea Horse

124th & 228th REGTS

GIFU

Hill 27

Mount Austen

▲▲▲▲▲ US front line, night of 10th January, 1943
△△△△△ Japanese positions 10th January
◄━━━ US attacks 10/18th January
•••••••• US front line, 18th January

Bottom map:

NIGHTS 1/2nd, 4/5th & 7/8th FEB. JAPANESE EVACUATE

Cape Esperance

0 Miles 6
0 Kilometres 10

Kamimbo Bay

Tenaro

N

9th FEB.

8th FEB.

Doma Cove

1st FEB. 2/132nd INF LANDS

Verahue

7th FEB.

Tassafaronga Pt.

4th FEB.

30th JAN.

26th JAN.

Pt Cruz

Kokumbona

23rd JAN.

G U A D A L C A N A L

Bonegi

Poha

Matanikau R.

Patch's offensive finally broke the Japanese line (top map), but he was too late to catch up with them before they evacuated (bottom map).

learned that it was advisable to halt any advance early in the afternoon, giving the troops time to dig in and for a general reconnaissance to be made in the daylight hours, as well as for the artillery observers to make their observations and determine the range. After some unpleasant and occasionally fatal 'shortfall' salvoes in the early days of the campaign, American troops had become nervous of their own artillery fire and it had become the practice of the forward observers to call down the first burst of fire well into the Japanese lines, drawing the fire back upon subsequent bursts.

It was accepted that movement had to be painfully slow. While trucks might achieve speeds of 20mph upon the few good roads, once these roads were left behind progress slowed to a crawl. Foot soldiers on jungle tracks might average one mile an hour; this was cut to half a mile or even a quarter of a mile an hour when inching through the jungle, hacking a path with a bayonet or a knife. Jeeps were able to make their way through most obstacles and trucks, although there were not enough of them, particularly the 2½ ton truck, were useful vehicles thanks to their powered front axles which were able to move over most forms of terrain. Some enterprising artillery units used mules as a form of transportation. Tanks could be useful, particularly in defence, but they were of limited use in the jungle where it was difficult to manouevre them. Japanese mines and anti-tank guns took a heavy toll of the light tanks used on Guadalcanal by the Americans.

Communications were always a problem. Radio sets tended to corrode, particularly voice radio sets, in the moist climate. Wherever possible troops relied on wired communication, although such apparatus could not always be taken right up to the front line. Sound powered telephones were discovered to be quite useful. Throughout the campaign close air-to-ground communication remained almost impossible and this made close air support strikes difficult.

American weapons were on the whole superior to those of the Japanese, especially in the later stages of the campaign. The MI (Garand) rifle was considered superior to the MI903 (Springfield) originally used, while of the sub-machine guns the .45 calibre Thompson was effective but sounded too much like some Japanese .25 calibre weapons and so could only be used sparingly at the front, particularly in night actions. The .30 calibre Browning automatic rifle was considered a good weapon and the .30 calibre machine guns, although heavy, were effective defensive weapons. Weight was an important consideration in the hand-to-hand fighting of which there was so much on Guadalcanal. It was just possible, for example to carry the 60mm mortar, but the heavier mortars presented a problem.

American artillery fire was a factor to be contended with on the island. The 105mm and the 155mm howitzers were both excellent. The Americans were great believers in softening up enemy positions with an intense artillery bombardment before sending in the infantry. Another commonly practised tactic was usually to skirt or pass any difficult pockets of resistance, isolate them and then come back and deal with them later.

Patch therefore possessed a considerable accumulation of data upon which to base any further action. He was also getting adequate supplies and ammunition for his forces. Auxiliary naval craft were filling the harbour at Tulagi, and Henderson Field was now an important strategic airbase and on its way to becoming even more so. As battle-weary and sick units were posted out, so fresh troops were coming in. The 5th Marines left on 9th December, followed by the 1st and then the 7th. The incidence of malaria alone in some units was as high as 75 per cent. Of the new troops coming to Guadalcanal a welcome arrival

Top left: An Army dugout about four miles west of Henderson Field. There were now many such positions on the island. *Bottom left:* Road-building was a hard job. *Above:* Vice-Admiral Kusaka

was Major-General Lawton Collins's 25th Infantry Division which had been diverted to the island while sailing from Hawaii to Sydney. This division came as the result of some horse-trading with MacArthur who received in return some of Vandegrift's marines, a bad bargain as it turned out for MacArthur because the marines would not be fit for combat duty for many months.

Also posted in to Guadalcanal were the 6th Marines under Colonel Gilder T Jackson, and units of the 2nd Division, bringing that division up to strength. In theory Patch's total force of three divisions came to 40,000 men, but some of his units were under strength. His air-power, however, was now considerable. The new Guadalcanal air commander, Brigadier-General Francis P Mulcahey, was in charge of what was now an all-weather airfield from which B-17s could fly missions to Rabaul, house twin-engined bombers and even a long-distance reconnaissance squadron of Lockheed Hudsons from New

143

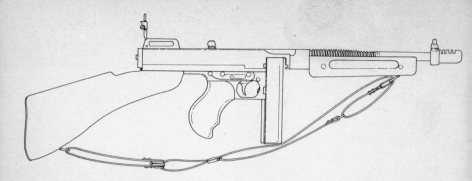

Thompson Caliber .45-inch Model 1928A1 Submachine gun. *Calibre:* .45-inch.
Method of operation: delayed blowback, selective fire. *Overall length:* 33.75 inches.
Barrel length: 10.5 inches. *Feed system:* 20- or 30-round staggered row detachable
box magazine, or 50-round drum. *Weight:* 10.75 lbs. *Muzzle velocity:* 920 feet per
second. *Cyclic rate of fire:* 600 to 725 rounds per minute. Later models were
produced without a compensator on the muzzle, simple L-type rear sight in place of
the adjustable leaf sight and radial cooling fins on the barrel. The main drawback of
the weapon was its complicated and precise manufacture, which resulted in the gun
not being as sturdy as it might, and also in high cost

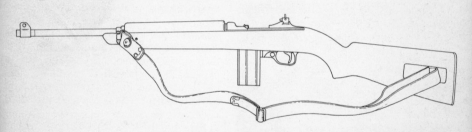

.30-inch M 1 Carbine. *Calibre:* .30-inch. *Method of operation:* gas, semi-automatic.
Overall length: 35.6 inches. *Barrel length:* 18 inches. *Feed system:* 15- or 30-round
staggered row detachable box magazine. *Weight:* 5.5 lbs. *Muzzle velocity:* 1,970
feet per second

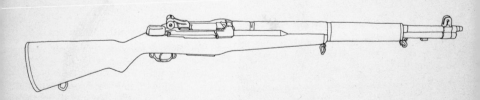

.30-inch M 1 Rifle (Garand semi-automatic rifle). *Calibre:* 30-inch. *Method of
operation:* gas, semi-automatic. *Overall length:* 43.6 inches. *Barrel length* 24 inches.
Feed system: 8-round staggered row non-detachable box magazine. *Weight:*
9.5 lbs. *Muzzle velocity:* 2,805 feet per second (firing M2 ball ammunition)

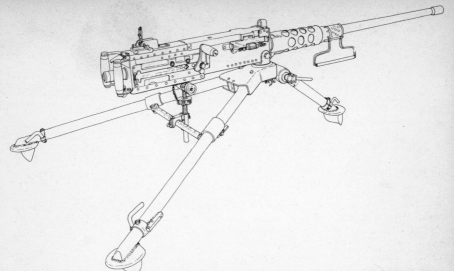

The standard heavy machine gun of the US Army, the Browning .5-inch machine gun was a formidable air-cooled weapon. The type was capable of firing a semi-armour piercing bullet, in which role the gun was used most often by the infantry. When mounted on a vehicle, the primary use of the gun was against aircraft.
Weight: 84 pounds. *Length:* 5 feet 5 inches. *Operation:* short recoil. *Rate of Fire:* 450 to 550 rounds per minute. *Muzzle velocity:* 3,050 fps (AP) and 2,930 fps (ball). *Range:* 6,470 yards (AP) and 7,460 yards (ball) maximum. Maximum effective range was about 2,000 yards. *Weight of bullet:* 1.71 ounces

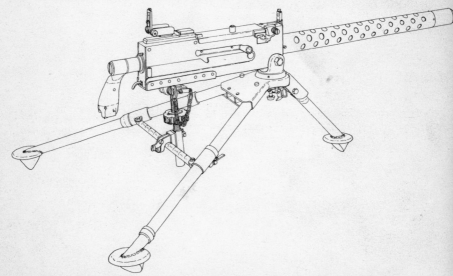

The .3-inch Browning was the US Army's standard infantry machine gun, an excellent air-cooled weapon. *Weight:* 31 pounds. *Length:* 3 feet 6 inches. *Operation:* short recoil. *Rate of fire:* 450 to 600 rounds per minute. *Muzzle Velocity:* 2,770 fps (AP) and 2,800 fps (ball). *Range:* 3,160 yards (AP) and 3,500 yards (ball) maximum. Maximum effective range was about 1,800 yards. *Weight of bullet:* .34 ounces

Left: Top brass on Guadalcanal, January 1943. Left to right: Secretary of the Navy Frank Knox, General Patch, Admiral Nimitz, Admiral Halsey, and General Collins. The campaign was now going well. *Above:* General Marston

Zealand. Not that the Japanese were completely a spent force in the air. On 7th December, for instance, they shot down the Marine dive-bomber leader, Major Joe Sailer. Sailer's reputation had been considerable. In five weeks he had flown twenty-five missions, made contact with the enemy on nineteen occasions, dropped his bombs on twelve of them and scored six hits and three near misses. He was shot down and killed while trying to bomb a Japanese destroyer.

By the beginning of January 1943, Patch could be satisfied with his force. All the land forces on Guadalcanal had been grouped under him in the newly formed XIV Corps. There had been some embarrassment when it was discovered that the 2nd Division Marine Commander, Major-General John Marston, was senior to Patch, but the latter had been promised the Guadalcanal command, so Marston turned over his command to his ADC, Brigadier-General Alphonse de Carre, and left the island. Patch's former post as commander of the Americal Division was given to Sebree.

On 10th January Patch decided that he was ready to march against Hyaku-

Left: Troops struggle along a trail as they help push the Japanese back.
Above: Kokumbuna beach in January

take west of the Matanikau. The only fly in the ointment was the fact that the Japanese on Mount Austen were still holding out, but Patch decided that a force could be detached to deal with this annoyance while the main strike was made to the west.

West of the Matanikau the Japanese, although starving and short of ammunition in many cases, were situated in strength between Point Cruz and Kokumbona. A series of strong-points had been linked by patrols and riflemen covering the areas between. At 0550 on 10th January the American artillery opened fire on the inland flank of the Japanese forces. For thirty minutes the heavy guns bombarded the Japanese lines with 6,000 rounds of ammunition. No sooner had the noise died away than twelve aircraft swooped over the Japanese lines, each dropping a quarter-of-a

ton bomb. Twelve SBDs followed, dropping 325 pound depth charges.

When the bombing was over, the American troops went forward. The 1st Battalion, 27th Infantry advanced on the area known as 'Galloping Horse'. To the left of 1st Battalion, the 3rd Battalion also went forward, encountering some opposition. Both battalions then dug in for the night. The same pattern was repeated the following morning. After an opening artillery fusilade the infantrymen went forward. This time the 3rd Battalion encountered trouble. Short of water (fresh supplies did not arrive until noon) men began to collapse in the heat. The battalion commander, Lieutenant-Colonel George E Bush, ordered his men to withdraw. As the Americans did so, the Japanese came forward with 90mm mortars, killing a number of the Americans.

The next morning the 3rd Battalion was pulled out of the line and replaced by the 2nd Battalion, commanded by Lt Col Herbert V Mitchell

Japanese positions on the western end of Guadalcanal get the heavy treatment

The battalion attacked up the southern slope of the 'Galloping Horse' area but was pinned down by accurate Japanese machine gun fire. It was a day of confusion but also of individual heroism. The two companies of the 2nd Battalion, existing without water for the greater part of the day, under constant fire from Japanese heavy and light machine guns, tried in vain to go forward. After a time the battalion Executive Officer, Captain Charles W Davis, managed to take a three-man patrol forward and locate the machine gun sites before returning.

On the following morning, 13th January, just before noon, Davis took another patrol forward, this time consisting of five men. They crept to within ten yards of the Japanese machine guns and then, watched by hundreds of Americans on adjacent ridges, charged the guns and put them out of action. Seeing this, the rest of the battalion also went forward and drove the Japanese from their position on 'Galloping Horse'.

It was during this campaign west of the Matanikau that another phrase went into the unofficial history of the Guadalcanal campaign. It was coined by Marine-Captain Henry Pierson Crow, in charge of a weapons company who discovered half a dozen marines cowering in a shell hole after a Japanese artillery attack. Pierson glowered at the marines and bellowed 'Goddamit, you'll never get a Purple Heart hiding in a foxhole! Follow me!' He then led the men in a charge against a Japanese position.

Meanwhile the Japanese were still holding out on Mount Austen. The men there were commanded by Colonel Oka and consisted of elements of battalions from the 124th and 228th Regiments and the 10th Mountain Artillery Regiment. They were entrenched in foxholes and pill boxes between two hills known as Hills 31 and 27. 500 men were occupying a horseshoe-shaped line of some forty-five fortifications. Each small fortification consisted of logs dug into the ground and covered with earth and foliage. One or two machine guns occupied each fortification and there were two or three riflemen in it as well. Outside the fortifications were supporting machine gunners and riflemen. The Japanese were in a strong defensive position, perhaps the strongest on Guadalcanal at this time, but all supplies and ammunition had to be brought to them through the besieging Americans. On 13th January a small party got through to Oka from General Hyakutake carrying supplies, but also bringing the orders of the general to surrender strongpoint 'Gifu' (so-called after a prefecture in Honshu). The order seems to have been ignored because the Japanese fought on. On 17th January the Americans broadcast messages through a loudspeaker, calling upon the Japanese to surrender. This demand was also ignored. The Americans then pressed their attack, pressing the Japanese back into a smaller area and finally overcoming the last opposition.

Hyakutake still had not received orders to evacuate his force from Guadalcanal. On 10th January, at the beginning of American push west of the Matanikau he had ordered the secret files of the Seventeenth Army to be destroyed and prepared to move his headquarters to the Tassafaronga area. Four days later reinforcements of a sort landed. This consisted of a small force of destroyers sent down the Slot by Rear-Admiral Koniji Koyanagi, who had taken over from Tanaka as Commander, Reinforcement Force. The destroyers were attacked by seven PT boats. The Japanese damaged two of the torpedo boats and managed to land the troops it had brought before retreating.

The force landed at Cape Esperance on 14th January included a party

which had not come to bring aid to the Japanese. It consisted of Lieutenant-Colonel Kumao Imoto and an escort who had brought the decision of the Japanese High Command to withdraw from Guadalcanal to Hyakutake. Each man in the expedition carried a 100 lb pack containing whisky, cigarettes, sweet cakes and dried fish to be distributed among the survivors. For eighteen hours Imoto and his men staggered past the corpses of men of the Seventh Army, eventually reaching the Japanese command post at the mouth of the Bonegi River. There Colonel Imoto delivered his message and the plans for the withdrawal to Colonel Haruo Konuma, the senior staff officer of the Seventh Army. Konuma, lying on a bed made of twigs in a blacked-out tent declared that the army did not even have the strength left for a withdrawal of the sort envisaged. He suggested that the survivors make one final charge, even if it was bound to fail. Imoto had no power to change the orders he had

been given and he was taken to see Hyakutake. The general was sitting on a blanket in a hole which had been dug for him under the roots of a large tree. He accepted the order for a withdrawal and the plans for its execution from Imoto, together with a personal letter from General Imamura. When Imoto had delivered his verbal message Hyakutake, who had been listening with closed eyes, said 'The question is very grave. I want to consider the matter quietly and alone for a little while. Please leave me alone until I call for you.'

At midday Imoto was ordered to return to General Hyakutake. The latter told the colonel that he would obey the orders and arrange for his troops to leave Guadalcanal. Later Hyakutake called a meeting of his staff officers and passed on the message to them. It was badly received. The officers wanted to make one final death or glory charge at the Americans Hyakutake replied that they must obey their orders from the High

Command.

Colonel Konuma was sent up to the front line on the afternoon of 17th January to inform Major-General Maruyama and Major-General Sano about the decision to abandon Guadalcanal. Only the senior officers knew of the decision. The rest of the army was told that any movements were merely to fresh defensive positions. On 15th January a battalion arrived from Rabaul and was sent up into the front line with the strongest of the remaining survivors. The rest of the veterans were slowly pulled back. At the same time Hyakutake and his staff made arrangements for the destruction or burial of artillery, ammunition and other supplies. Destroyers landed more supplies of food and these were stored at various points, especially at Kokumbona, Tassafaronga, Kamimbo and Cape Esperance. Wounded were also transported to Cape Esperance to be loaded on board the destroyers.

Slowly the Japanese fell back, followed by the Americans. By 18th

A final stand. US troops overran this machine-gun nest shortly before the Japanese withdrawal from Guadalcanal

January Patch ordered the American position a little over half a mile west of the Matanikau to be consolidated. The fighting was almost over, although it was not officially to end until the middle of February, but the Americans were to be reminded that the Japanese were dangerous adversaries as long as they could fight. On 1st February Patch decided to send a detachment of troops up the coast to Verahue in order to cut off some of the retreating Japanese. The force consisted of the 2nd Battalion, 132nd Infantry and some personnel detached from the 3rd Battalion as well as artillery, communications, medical and engineering personnel. This force was loaded on to ships at Kukum and successfully unloaded at Verahue. On the way back from escorting this force, however, the destroyer *De Haven*

153

was attacked and sent to the bottom in a heavy Japanese air attack in full view of many American troops on the shore.

The air attack was part of a Japanese plan to make the Americans think that the enemy were about to launch another full scale attack on Guadalcanal and to provide a cloak for the imminent withdrawal. On 30th January a Japanese task force including two aircraft carriers, two battleships and a dozen other warships left Truk apparently making for Guadalcanal. Towards the end of January coast-watchers also reported the accumulation of a large force of Japanese ships at Rabaul and in the Shortlands.

Both Halsey and Patch came to the conclusion that the Japanese had hoped they would. The American commanders assumed that the Japanese were about to make a spectacular effort to invade Guadalcanal and reinforce the Seventeenth Army. Patch called back some of his forces to guard Henderson Field and stopped pressing home the full force of his attack upon the Japanese west of the Matanikau. This was just what the Japanese had been hoping for. They had been clinging desperately to the coastal tracks around Cape Esperance and now it was possible for them to embark upon the destroyers, the last famous run of the Tokyo Express now coming down from Rabaul. The Americans knew nothing of what was happening. As a Japanese commander said later 'It is still one of the miracles of the war to me that this should have remained such a successful secret. The marvel of this increases when one considers that the enemy enjoyed absolute supremacy of the air in the vicinity of Guadalcanal at this time.'

At 2130 on 1st February, the first of 2,316 Japanese, the remainder of General Sano's force, once 8,000 strong, boarded the barges off Cape Esperance. Before midnight they were on some of the twenty-two destroyers to be used in the evacuation and were steaming into the night. Three nights later it was the turn of what was left of Saruyama's Sendai Division to leave Guadalcanal. The same night Hyakutake and the senior members of his staff went on board the destroyer *Hamakaze*. Hyakutake greeted the captain of the vessel briefly and then went below to his cabin. He did not emerge as the destroyer steamed away from Guadalcanal. On 7th February the rearguard under Colonel Matsuda, some 3,000 men, left from Kamimbo. The crew of the destroyers picking them up were horrified, as had been the sailors on the other vessels, at the state of the soldiers, emaciated, fever-ridden and suffering from intense battle-weariness, dreadful wounds and malnutrition. Nevertheless, the evacuation had been a magnificent success. In three nights the Japanese Navy had picked up and taken away between 11,000 and 12,000 men.

The Americans discovered what had happened, but by then it was too late. It must have been some small consolation to the Japanese that after all they had suffered on Guadalcanal the last great tactical success had been theirs. As Admiral Nimitz was to admit somewhat ruefully in his Action Report of 17th April, 1943: 'Until almost the last moment it appeared that the Japanese were attempting a major reinforcement effort. Only skill in keeping their plans disguised and bold celerity in carrying them out enabled the Japanese to withdraw the remnants of the Japanese garrison. Not until after all organized forces had been evacuated on 8th February did we realise the purpose of their air and naval dispositions; otherwise with the strong forces available to us on Guadalcanal and our powerful fleet in the South Pacific, we might have converted the withdrawal into a disastrous rout.'

It was a generous tribute and a deserved one.

Grisly testimony to the savagery of Japanese resistance

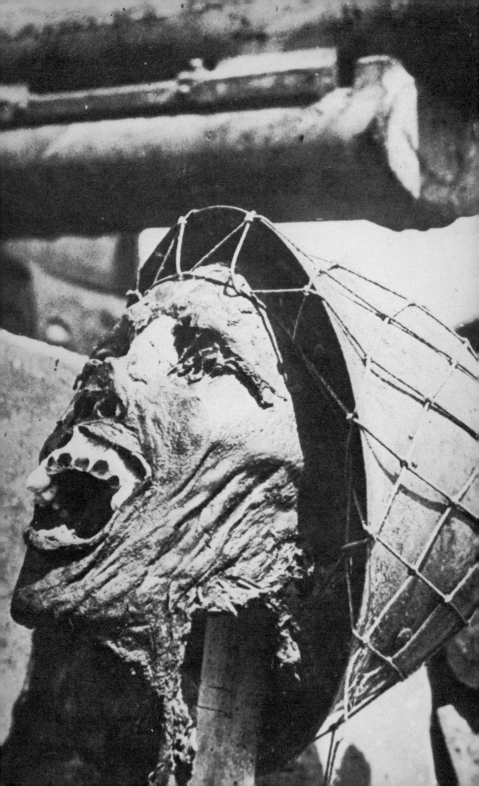

Aftermath

The land fighting on Guadalcanal officially ended in the middle of February, although small groups of Japanese were still being encountered long after this. Indeed, the last Japanese soldier to surrender on Guadalcanal did so on 27th October, 1947, four and a half years after the fighting was over and two years after the war had ended! His only belongings were a water bottle, a broken Australian bayonet and a Japanese

Henderson Field in 1944. A vast air base has been built on the muddy strip the Marines captured in 1942

entrenching shovel.

Guadalcanal remained an Allied base until the end of the war. Henderson Field was used for long-distance bombing raids and as a jumping-off area for ground troops. The war in the Solomons did not end until August, 1945. After Guadalcanal the Japanese had to be cleared off the Russell Islands and then out of Choiseul and New Georgia in the Western Solomons.

The name Guadalcanal remained a synonym for desperate fighting. For years after the end of hostilities the skeletons of Japanese soldiers continued to be discovered. The island became one huge ammunition dump; today, more than a quarter-century later, bombs and ammunition are still being defused and otherwise rendered harmless. The island also remains famous for many tales of heroism and gallant conduct on both sides. Among the American forces, the following medals were awarded: 5 Medals of Honour; 113 Navy Crosses; 4 DSMs; 3 DSOs (British); 2 Conspicuous Gallantry Medals.

Guadalcanal is also generally recognized as having been the turning point of the war in the Pacific. On the American side, General George Marshall, the Army Chief of Staff, said: 'The resolute defence of these marines and the desperate gallantry of our naval task forces marked the turning point in the Pacific.' His sentiments were echoed by a number of senior Japanese officers. Major-General Kawabe, Deputy Chief of the Army General Staff said: 'As to the turning point, when the positive action ceased or even became negative, it was, I feel, at Guadalcanal.' Captain Ohmae, the Rabaul naval tactician, agreed: 'After Guadalcanal I knew we could not win the war. I did not think we would lose, but I knew we could not win.'

The American victory on the island provided them with a number of advantages. The Japanese had been shown to be fallible; their navy, although a force to be reckoned with, did not emerge in battle formation for several years; the Americans were provided with a springboard for their hops across the Pacific; in addition the Japanese had lost thousands of men and much material on

Guadalcanal, as well as hundreds of aircraft and irreplaceable pilots. After Guadalcanal, the Japanese did not advance again. They fought stubbornly, often heroically, but all the time they were going backwards.

There were other after-effects, especially among the Solomon Islanders. During the war, although having little idea of what it was all about, they were true to the Allied cause, helping in many ways. The islanders even had their own song, sung in Pidgin, the *lingua franca* of the Solomons, in which they poked fun at their Japanese conquerors. The song was called *Japani Ha-ha* and each verse ended with the refrain, 'Me laugh along you, Japani, ha-ha.' But not all the results of the war were amusing. Solomon Islanders were killed in bombing raids, their homes were destroyed and gardens ruined. Even so, the most lasting effect of the conflict was perhaps the sight of their British masters, so long regarded as all-powerful, fleeing from the Japanese advance. The fact, too, that it was the Americans who reconquered the island, not the British, was noticed and remembered. The Americans turned out to be generous and easy-going; their treatment of

Above: A boat-load of Marines comes ashore in the Russell Islands
Opposite: The ordeal of Guadalcanal

coloured people seemed. by Solomon Islands standards, generous. After the war was over a cult started which claimed that the Americans were coming back soon, laden with presents for the islanders. When these presents did not materialise the islanders became sulky and obstructive. Eventually this culminated in the movement known as Marching Rule, which had to be put down by a show of force.

Tulagi never again became the government headquarters. The British administration took over the site of an American base on Guadalcanal and established the town of Honiara there; this is now the capital of the Solomons. In remote villages there are still reminders of the war; most village schools have an empty shell case for use as the school bell; Japanese swords are used as digging implements; helmets make bowls. Some names remain from the war years – Red Beach, Ironbottom Sound, and others; they are reminders of the time when a remote South Pacific island became the bloody centre of a war.

Bibliography

The Coastwatchers by Eric Feldt (Pacific Books, London. Tri-Ocean, San Francisco)
The Quadalcanal Campaign by John L Zimmerman (Historical Division Headquarters, US Marine Corps)
History of Marine Corps Aviation in World War II by Robert Sherrod (Combat Forces Press, Washington DC)
Condition Red: Destroyer Action in the South Pacific by Frederick J Bell (Longmans, London)
Follow Me: the Story of the Second Marine Division in World War II by Richard W Johnston (Random House, New York)
Battle for Guadalcanal by Samuel Griffith (Lippincott, New York)
Among those Present: The Official Story of the Pacific Islands at War (Central Office of Information, London)
The Pacific: Guadalcanal to Saipan: The Army Air Forces in World War II by W F Craven and J L Cate (Air Force Historical Division, Chicago)